BUILDING SECURE AND TRANSPARENT SYSTEMS

ADB'S BLOCKCHAIN INITIATIVES IN ASIA AND THE PACIFIC

MAY 2026

ASIAN DEVELOPMENT BANK

ADB

6 ADB Avenue, Mandaluyong City, 1550 Metro Manila, Philippines
Tel +63 2 8632 4444; Fax +63 2 8636 2444
www.adb.org

ISBN 978-92-9277-785-2 (print); 978-92-9277-786-9 (PDF); 978-92-9277-787-6 (ebook)
Publication Stock No. SPR260163-2
DOI: http://dx.doi.org/10.22617/SPR260163-2

Notes:
In this publication, "$" refers to United States dollars.
ADB recognizes "China" as the People's Republic of China; "Hong Kong" as Hong Kong, China; and "Vietnam" as Viet Nam.
All photos in this publication are from the Asian Development Bank unless otherwise stated.

Cover design by Mike Cortes

Contents

Tables and Figures

Tables

Figures

Foreword

Emerging technologies continue to reshape the way we think about trust, transparency, and efficiency in systems that serve people and communities. While the hype surrounding blockchains has somewhat subsided, its potential nonetheless remains the same: it can decentralize data, automate transactions, and reduce reliance on intermediaries, offering new ways to deliver services more securely and inclusively while potentially offering cost savings.

That being said, blockchain is not a silver bullet. Like any technology, it has limitations. If used properly and in the right context, however, and in collaboration with key stakeholders, it can be a powerful tool for good—enhancing traceability, lowering costs, and expanding access to underserved populations.

Part of our work at the Information Technology Department of the Asian Development Bank (ADB) involves exploring how innovative technologies such as blockchain can be harnessed to help improve ADB's operational efficiency and support developing member countries. Through the Digital Innovation Sandbox Program, we, together with our colleagues from other ADB departments, have taken an iterative, hands-on approach to testing blockchain across a range of use cases in safe—but real-world—environments.

Our pilots have spanned sectors and geographies, including streamlining trade finance between Thailand and Viet Nam, modernizing land leasing in Fiji, and enabling carbon trading platforms in Bhutan and the People's Republic of China. We have also tested how blockchain can support cross-border securities transactions, digitize certificates of origin in Mongolia, and experiment with using non-fungible tokens for marine conservation fundraising in Indonesia. Through these initiatives, we saw the potential of blockchain to improve operational efficiency, reduce risks, and make systems more inclusive. We also saw that beyond technology, stakeholder engagement can spell the difference between success and failure.

This compendium brings together our experiences—what worked, what did not, and what we learned along the way. We share these lessons with the hope that these will spark dialogue, inspire collaboration, and encourage continued experimentation with technologies that can help shape a more prosperous, inclusive, resilient, and sustainable Asia and the Pacific.

Stephanie KC Hung
Director General
Information Technology Department
Asian Development Bank

Acknowledgments

Building Secure and Transparent Systems: ADB's Blockchain Initiatives in Asia and the Pacific was developed by the Information Technology Department of the Asian Development Bank.

Marc Lepage, principal IT specialist for technology innovation at the Information Technology Department, guided the development of this publication. Melanie Sison prepared the case studies and led the production of the publication.

Special thanks go to colleagues, particularly Jean-Baptiste Mounier, Masato Nakane, Ritchie Roño, Satoru Yamadera, Seok Yong Yoon, Shamit Chakravarti, Stephen Beck, and Takeru Toba, for providing technical input and feedback on the documentation of initiatives that involved their respective offices. Consultants Christopher Verceles and James Ball provided valuable insights on blockchain that contributed to the development of this publication.

This publication was produced with the support of colleagues from the Information Technology Department and the Department of Communications and Knowledge Management.

Abbreviations

ADB	Asian Development Bank
API	application programming interface
ASEAN	Association of Southeast Asian Nations
ASEAN+3	ASEAN, the People's Republic of China, Japan, and the Republic of Korea
ASYCUDA	Automated System for Customs Data
COO	certificate of origin
COVID-19	coronavirus disease
CSD	central securities depository
DVP	delivery versus payment
ICE	Indonesian Cyber Education
MNCCI	Mongolia National Chamber of Commerce and Industry
MVP	minimum viable product
NFT	non-fungible token
POC	proof of concept
PRC	People's Republic of China
RTGS	real-time gross settlement
RWA	real-world asset
SMEs	small and medium-sized enterprises
TLTB	iTaukei Land Trust Board

Glossary

Blockchain	type of distributed ledger technology that batches transaction history into "blocks," with each successive block referencing the previous block with a hash pointer and a Merkle root of its transactions, forming a tamper-evident chain (thus, "blockchain")
Consensus mechanism	automatically coordinates and ensures the consistency of data across nodes. This contributes to the "trustlessness" of blockchains: the system gives users the assurance that the data is reliable and accurate.
Distributed ledger technology	digital system that uses cryptography and peer-to-peer networking to record, verify, and synchronize data, including asset ownership and transfers
Hash	string of characters that serves as the tamper-evident seal
Non-fungible token	type of digital asset, with the proof of ownership or authenticity of these unique items or pieces of content stored on a digital ledger
Oracle	Third-party service or secure middleware that connects blockchain-based smart contracts with "off-chain" data sources
Proof-of-work	consensus algorithm where participants compete to solve complex mathematical puzzles. The first to solve the puzzle gets to validate the next block of transactions and receives a reward.
Proof-of-stake	consensus algorithm wherein participants are selected by how much stake they have
Smart contract	programmable application deployed on distributed ledger technology that executes complex business logic autonomously; can interact with other contracts to create composable systems, integrate real-world data through oracles, and implement sophisticated economic mechanisms

Executive Summary

Blockchain is a decentralized digital system for recording transactions across multiple nodes in a network. It holds transformative potential for addressing persistent development challenges in Asia and the Pacific, a region that faces complex challenges such as fragmented markets, inefficient public service delivery, and limited financial inclusion. Blockchain offers a technological foundation to overcome these barriers by enabling secure, transparent, and automated systems that reduce costs, improve accountability, and foster cross-border collaboration.

This publication presents initiatives supported by the Asian Development Bank (ADB), through the Digital Innovation Sandbox Program, that demonstrate how blockchain could be leveraged to address some of these challenges across different contexts.

In the People's Republic of China, ADB supported the development of a blockchain-based carbon trading platform to address inefficiencies in the national emissions trading scheme. The initiative demonstrated how blockchain can improve transparency, reduce double counting of carbon credits, and enable seamless integration between domestic and international carbon markets.

ADB also supported the development of a minimum viable product of a blockchain-based carbon credit issuance platform in Bhutan. The initiative showed how the technology could automate verification processes and reduce transaction costs.

To enhance financial integration in the Association of Southeast Asian Nations, the People's Republic of China, Japan, and the Republic of Korea, ADB's Project Tridecagon tested the use of blockchain for cross-border securities transactions. The initiative demonstrated the feasibility of connecting different blockchains into one network, potentially reducing settlement risks and improving regional capital market efficiency.

In trade finance, ADB piloted a blockchain-based platform to digitize credit guarantee transactions that culminated in a live transaction between institutions in Thailand and Viet Nam. The transaction showed how blockchain could modernize trade finance while reducing processing time and operational risk.

In Maldives and Mongolia, blockchain was trialed for streamlining trade documentation—specifically certificates of origin and customs processes—with the aim of reducing fraud, improving efficiency, and supporting the establishment of national single window systems. The Maldives initiative was parked for future consideration.

In Fiji, ADB's Information Technology Department supported the expansion of a blockchain-based platform that improved transparency and reduced processing times for customary land leases. This included the development of a proof-of-concept of a mobile voting feature that would allow landowners to provide their consent digitally to make customary land available for lease.

Meanwhile, ADB also supported two blockchain initiatives in Indonesia. One was on the development of a digital credentialing system for online education in Indonesia, which enhanced trust and portability of academic records. Another tested the use of non-fungible tokens to explore alternative fundraising mechanisms for conservation.

Executive Summary

By fostering innovation and supporting digital transformation, ADB helps its developing member countries harness the power of emerging technologies to address complex development challenges and improve the lives of people across Asia and the Pacific.

This publication also features snippets of think pieces from thought leaders of ADB and industry discussing blockchain in relation to the challenges and opportunities in Asia and the Pacific.

Blockchain's key feature. Blockchain can provide a shared and tamper-resistant system for recording transactions across multiple participants.

CHAPTER 1
Blockchain: An Overview

This chapter explains what blockchain is and how it uses smart contracts. It also provides examples of how blockchain is applied in various contexts.

What is Blockchain?

Blockchain is a digital system that uses cryptography and peer-to-peer networking to record, verify, and synchronize data across a distributed network of users. A blockchain system retains identical copies of a shared, append-only ledger.[1] The transaction history is stored into "blocks," each secured and linked to the previous block via cryptographic hashes, strings of characters that serve as tamper-evident seals (thus, "blockchain").[2] New blocks are formed when data is added, and this append-only structure ensures corrections can only occur through new transactions. Each successive block references the previous block with a hash pointer and a Merkle root, which summarizes all the transaction data stored within the block.

The consensus mechanism is a critical element of blockchain. This is the process by which nodes running the protocol software across a distributed network agree on the validity and ordering of transactions recorded on a shared ledger, reducing dependence on a single trusted intermediary.[3] Reversing committed transactions which have been added to the ledger after consensus has been achieved becomes either economically prohibitive or if the consensus and finality model is deterministic, effectively impossible under standard conditions.

The consensus mechanism serves as a security mechanism that helps prevent malicious actors from hijacking the ledger. This contributes to the "trustlessness" of blockchains: the system reduces the need to trust any single participant, as the protocol itself enforces the integrity of the ledger.[4]

Features of Blockchain

Blockchain's key features include the following:

(i) **Automated verification processes.** Blockchain significantly reduces manual efforts as it automates at least some core steps in business processes. This includes validating data and storing the history of transactions in the participants' respective ledgers, which reduces the need for manual reconciliations or duplicated records. Leveraging smart contracts deployed on public ledgers, users can automatically verify that predefined conditions are met before executing transactions.

(ii) **Peer-to-peer.** Blockchain's peer-to-peer setup eliminates the need for an intermediary—such as a bank—to validate, process, and authenticate transactions. This potentially reduces transactional costs and settlement

Figure 1: Data Storage in Blockchains

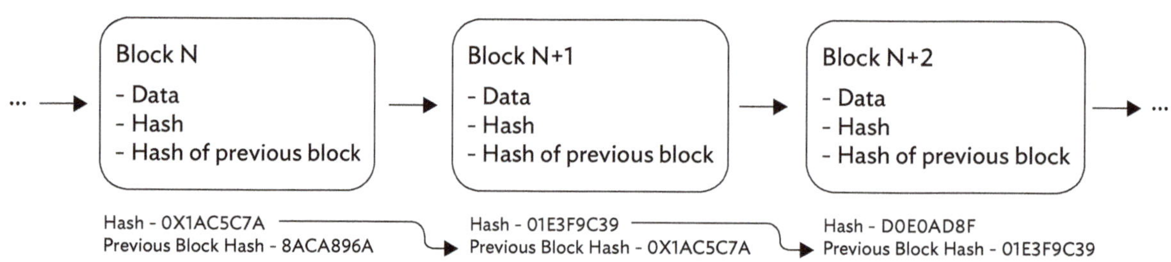

Note: In a blockchain, data is stored in blocks, which are connected to each other via cryptographic hashes. Change any block and all following hashes break, exposing tampering. This is an important feature of a blockchain, providing a strong, temporally consistent immutable record of information.

Source: Asian Development Bank.

1 B. Ferrarini, J. Maupin, and M. Hinojales. 2017. Distributed Ledger Technologies for Developing Asia. *ADB Economics Working Paper Series*. No. 533. Asian Development Bank (ADB).

2 World Bank. 2017. Distributed Ledger Technology (DLT) and Blockchain. *FinTech Note*. No. 1.

3 S. Seibold and G. Samman. Consensus: Immutable Agreement for the Internet of Value. *KPMG*.

4 R. Huang, X. Yang, and P. Ajay. 2023. Consensus Mechanism for Software-defined Blockchain in Internet of Things. *Internet of Things and Cyber-Physical Systems*. 3. pp. 52–60.

frictions as two or more parties can transact directly with each other.

(iii) **Improved security.** Transactions, once recorded, cannot be altered or deleted. This makes the system tamper resistant and less vulnerable to fraud. In addition, all transactions are reflected in the ledger, making transactions transparent, verifiable, and auditable. Each transaction is cryptographically secured and time-stamped with a digital signature, creating a tamper-proof and immutable audit trail. Furthermore, new information is reflected in the ledger in real time, adding a layer of transparency and reducing risk. In addition, the data is more resilient against cyberattacks because identical copies of the ledger are maintained across geographically distributed nodes, each secured by cryptographic hashing and digital signatures. Changes to the transaction history require approval through a consensus algorithm, meaning no single compromised node can unilaterally alter the record. This effectively means that there is no single point of failure because the data is distributed across these nodes.

(iv) **Interoperability.** Standardized blockchain systems may communicate, share data, and interact with each other, enabling broader collaboration and innovation across platforms.

(v) **"Trustless."** Blockchain participants do not have to reverify data from any given network. Instead, they mutually agree on the cryptographically secure state of the written record on the ledger rather than their counterparties without having to know or trust each other.[5]

(vi) **Redundancy.** Blockchain is distributed by nature and can be decentralized virtually and geographically. This gives the system a high degree of redundancy in scenarios where systems fail.

Thus, blockchain offers various advantages over traditional databases, as it ensures that data is immutable, transparent, and verifiable, and shared across multiple stakeholders in real time. These characteristics make blockchain particularly well-suited for multiparty applications requiring trust, traceability, and efficiency. However, blockchain is not always a silver bullet solution. For example, in instances where a single trusted operator suffices, data rarely changes hands, or low latency is essential, a conventional database is a simpler and cheaper solution.

Types of Blockchain Networks

Blockchains can be classified according to the purpose for which these networks are built.

Public networks, as indicated by their name, allow anyone to join and participate. These are often described as "permissionless" because there is no central authority governing access and consensus is incentivized through shared economic security and alignment, typically via "proof-of-work," which is the consensus algorithm wherein participants compete to solve complex mathematical puzzles, or "proof-of-stake," which is the consensus algorithm wherein participants are selected based on how much stake they have. This quality gives public blockchains very strong censorship resistance properties.

In contrast, private networks are overseen by parties that control who can join and participate in the network. Consortium networks, meanwhile, are composed of multiple organizations that share the responsibility of maintaining the network—while they do not have a single point of control, they are not fully open.[6]

The choice of network type is application-dependent, as it typically involves tradeoffs between privacy, decentralization, scalability, and control. The tamper resistance or immutability of a chain depends on assumed adversary, honest-majority thresholds, and cost to attack (hash power, stake, or collusion between validators).

---

5 IBM. Benefits of Blockchain; and BCB Group. 2022. What Does Trustless Mean in Crypto? 4 October.

6 S. Susnjara and I. Smalley. What is Blockchain? *Think* newsletter. IBM.

Figure 2: Blockchain Network Types by Access and Governance

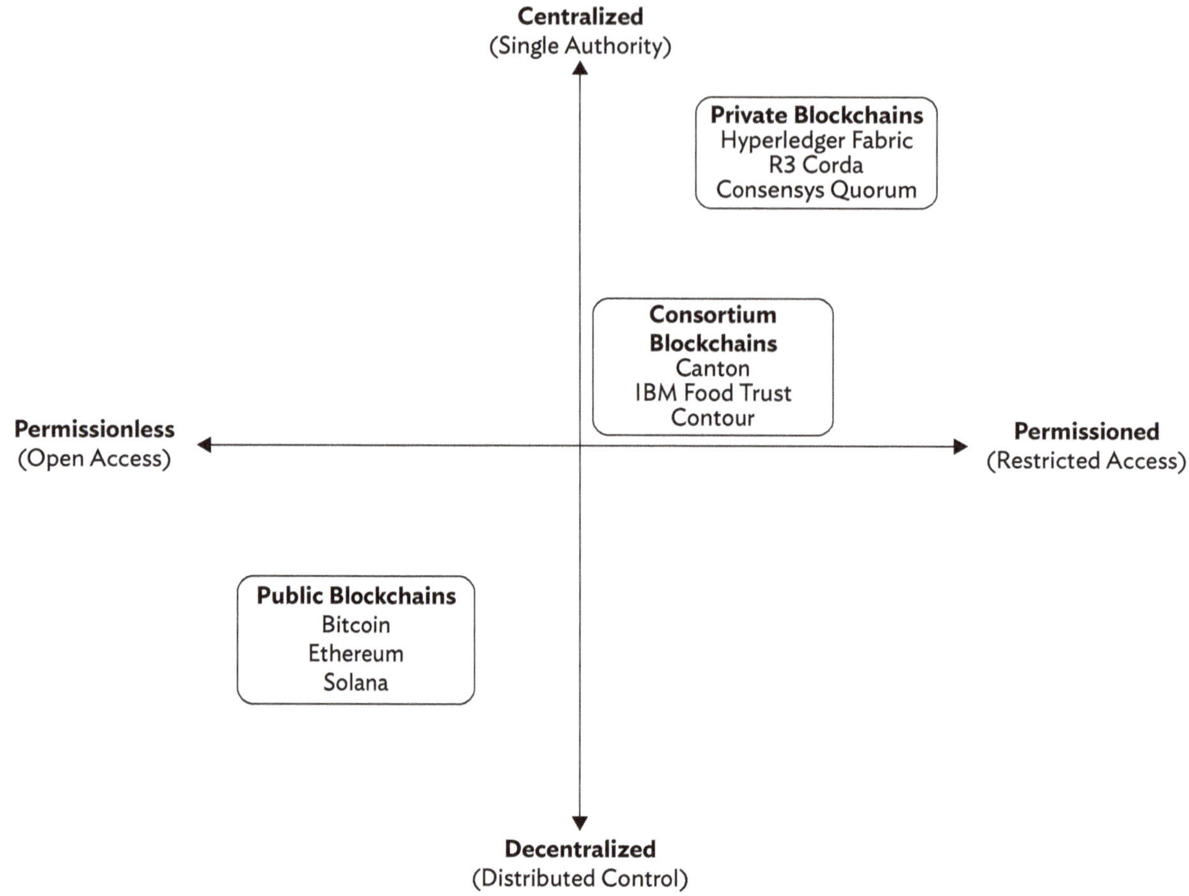

Source: Asian Development Bank.

Blockchain and Smart Contracts

Smart contracts are programmable applications deployed on blockchains that can execute complex business logic autonomously. Smart contracts can interact with other contracts to create composable systems, enabling them to "talk" with each other. These interactions can include integrating real-world data through oracles, which are trusted mechanisms that bring "off-chain" data to the blockchain, and implement sophisticated economic mechanisms, such as automated price determination using algorithms. Smart contracts transform static agreements into dynamic and responsive systems that can adapt to changing conditions; examples of applications built with smart contracts include asset tokenization, and complex multiparty delivery versus payment (DVP) settlement systems. Note that not all blockchains support smart contract functionality.

Blockchain and Development

Blockchain is closely associated with finance, but it is increasingly being used across various industries, allowing these industries to become embedded and interoperate closely and efficiently within each other. The true power of blockchain emerges not just from its application within individual sectors, but from its ability to create a shared trust infrastructure across industries. Digital trust acts as a connective fiber, enabling previously siloed industries to interact seamlessly.

For instance, a single blockchain system can simultaneously handle supply chain verification, trade finance, insurance claims, and regulatory compliance, creating an interconnected ecosystem where data flows securely between health care providers, insurers, and regulators, or where agricultural products can be traced from farm to table while automatically triggering smart insurance payouts for weather events and facilitating cross-border payments. Examples of these applications include the following:

(i) **Trade.** Blockchain is being used to support cross-border payments and make trade finance faster and more efficient (footnote 1).
(ii) **Supply chain management.** Blockchain improves supply chain management by enabling stakeholders to use the same secure ledger to track goods from origin to consumer. The transparency offered by the technology has the potential to lower corruption risks.[7]
(iii) **Asset management.** With blockchain serving as a single source of truth, asset records can be safely stored on the digital ledger to make it easy to trace and manage ownership of tangible and intangible assets.
(iv) **Insurance.** Insurance notes and contracts can be immutably registered and traded on a public digital ledger, allowing for more streamlined access to insurance markets, and providing policyholders with faster access to payouts.
(v) **Social protection.** Records and credentials may be safely stored on the digital ledger, enabling individuals to have greater control over their personal data while giving the means to enjoy better access to services. In addition, blockchain can help aid organizations and nongovernment organizations track assistance to poor and vulnerable communities.[8] One example is Building Blocks, a World Food Programme project that streamlines assistance from different humanitarian organizations using blockchain to make cash transfers more efficient, secure, and transparent.[9]
(vi) **Health care.** Blockchain provides health care facilities the means to maintain and share health records in a secure manner.
(vii) **Energy and the environment.** Blockchain provides a secure transaction settlement ledger, enabling smaller-scale power producers and consumers to interact with a distributed power grid. It also provides tamper-evident reporting for environmental, social, and governance disclosures.

[7] Deutsche Gesellschaft für Internationale Zusammenarbeit. 2020. *The Potential of Distributed Ledger Technologies in the Fight Against Corruption*.

[8] Blockchain Council. 2023. Blockchain for Social Impact: Driving Positive Change Through Distributed Ledger Technology. 18 July.

[9] World Food Programme. Building Blocks.

Blockchain in trade and finance. Blockchain can support the modernization of trade and finance processes.

CHAPTER 2
Blockchain for Trade and Finance

Blockchain is being explored as a tool to modernize trade and finance systems, including improving the efficiency of cross-border transactions. Its potential lies in creating more resilient, interoperable financial infrastructure that supports regional integration while respecting national systems and regulatory frameworks.

Blockchain and cross-border settlements. Blockchain can enable faster and more secure cross-border securities settlement by linking key market infrastructures across economies.

The Asian Bond Markets Initiative was launched in 2002 by the finance ministers of the Association of Southeast Asian Nations, the People's Republic of China, Japan, and the Republic of Korea (ASEAN+3) to boost the development of local currency bond markets, with ADB acting as the Asian Bond Markets Initiative secretariat since its inception. The Cross-Border Settlement Infrastructure Forum, whose members are central securities depositories (CSDs) and central banks in ASEAN+3, was created to enhance dialogues among policymakers and bond operators. Ways to improve bond and cash settlement infrastructure in the region are covered in these discussions.[10]

One of the discussion topics covered establishing regional settlement intermediary options to address regional market impediments to link key market settlement infrastructures of ASEAN+3 more effectively and efficiently. This would also support the efficient utilization of local currency bonds as collateral, which, in turn, would increase local currency liquidity in times of market stress in ASEAN+3. However, Asian economies require at least 1 trade day plus 2 working days for these cross-border transactions to be processed under the current market practices through correspondent banking networks, although they are located in the

Blockchain-Based Digital Regional Settlement Intermediary Platform in the Association of Southeast Asian Nations, the People's Republic of China, Japan, and the Republic of Korea
Making cross-border settlement of bond transactions quicker and safer

Highlights

- Intra-regional securities transactions may take days because the current operational practices are handled by various financial intermediaries with differing operating hours.
- ADB's Project Tridecagon developed a proof-of-concept (POC) that leveraged blockchain to execute cross-border delivery-versus-payment of cash and securities transactions.

Fast Facts

Economies: Association of Southeast Asian Nations, the People's Republic of China, Japan, and the Republic of Korea (ASEAN+3)
Years of implementation: 2021–2022
Information Technology Department's partner ADB department: Economic Research and Development Impact Department
ADB's External Partners: Consensys, R3, Soramitsu, Fujitsu (technology service providers)

10 ADB. 2014. *Basic Principles on Establishing a Regional Settlement Intermediary and Next Steps Forward: Cross-Border Settlement Infrastructure Forum*; and Independent Evaluation Department. 2021. *Creating a Regional Settlement Intermediary in ASEAN+3: Cross-Border Settlement Infrastructure Forum*. ADB.

same or similar time zone. The time lag between a trade agreement and the settlement of securities and money cannot eliminate settlement risks.[11] In addition, developing a centralized regional infrastructure consisting of national financial market infrastructures was deemed costly and could not escape from the issue of geopolitical hegemony.

The idea of CSD–real-time gross settlement (RTGS) linkages proposed by the Cross-Border Settlement Infrastructure Forum can avoid the issue of hegemony and ensure sovereignty; thus, the Bank of Japan and Hong Kong Monetary Authority established the link in 2021, along with the Cross-Border Settlement Infrastructure Forum discussion. However, a host-to-host linkage is too costly to implement in developing markets. Against this backdrop, ADB explored whether innovative decentralized technologies with blockchain could be used to make processing transactions more efficient for developing markets even with the current legal and regulatory systems in place.

As early as 2014, many ASEAN+3 members saw the CSD-RTGS linkage model as the model that best addresses their requirements for a regional settlement intermediary.[12] It uses a flexible implementation approach that enables cross-border and cross-currency bond settlement in DVP using central bank money to mitigate settlement risks and encourage cross-border transactions and investments. This model assumes that only CSDs and central banks interact in cases of cross-border settlements, and this premise was carried over in this initiative, dubbed Project Tridecagon.[13]

Project Tridecagon was a proof-of-concept (POC) that tested whether key market infrastructures across ASEAN+3—central banks' RTGS and CSDs' book-entry systems—could be connected using innovative technology. It sought to connect three economic models to reflect the financial environment in ASEAN+3, which is composed of countries with different frameworks, systems, and policies. Specifically, it aimed to determine whether it was possible to connect three different blockchain platforms to perform an atomic swap of three tokens (foreign currency, local currency, and security tokens) to simulate the real-world environment wherein heterogeneity of blockchain-based platforms and economic models are expected across countries.[14] The intent was not to show that blockchain could replace the existing legacy systems but rather to show that it could coexist with these, as the technology was seen to have a huge potential to streamline the process of cross-border financial transactions. It is worth noting that Project Tridecagon leverages R3 Corda. While Corda is technically a distributed ledger technology rather than a traditional blockchain, this report uses the term "blockchain" as a catch-all for these technologies for the sake of simplicity.

ADB screened and invited technology service providers that had experience in and exposure to similar initiatives. The selected firms were assigned to develop blockchain-based platforms based on the following economic models:

(i) **Model Economy A.** The RTGS and book-entry systems are separate ledgers of different tokens, with the central bank running the former and the CSD responsible for securities. This is based on the system followed by the People's Republic of China (PRC), the Republic of Korea, Malaysia, the Philippines, and Thailand. R3 was tasked with developing the Economy A model using Corda as its blockchain solution.

[11] ADB. 2023. *Connecting Market Infrastructures in ASEAN+3: The Project Tridecagon Proof of Concept*.

[12] ADB. 2014. *Basic Principles on Establishing a Regional Settlement Intermediary and Next Steps Forward: Cross-Border Settlement Infrastructure Forum*.

[13] While the POC was a simulation, it still respected the sovereignty of central banks. Thus, one of the assumptions of this initiative was that only the central bank could mint local currency cash tokens. In addition, the CSDs were considered the only party that could mint securities tokens based on account holder information.

[14] "Atomic swap" is the term used to describe the instantaneous exchange of digital assets.

(ii) **Model Economy B.** The RTGS and the government bond book-entry system are under one ledger of the central bank. This is the model that is used by Hong Kong, China; Indonesia; Japan; and Singapore. Soramitsu used Hyperledger Iroha 2.0 to develop a blockchain-based platform for this model.

(iii) **Model Economy C.** In contrast to model economies A and B, this is a hypothetical model based on the premise that an economy can run full-scale blockchain payment and securities settlement systems. Consensys, using Ethereum, was tapped to develop this model.

Figure 3: How Blockchain Can Potentially Support International or Domestic Settlement Flows

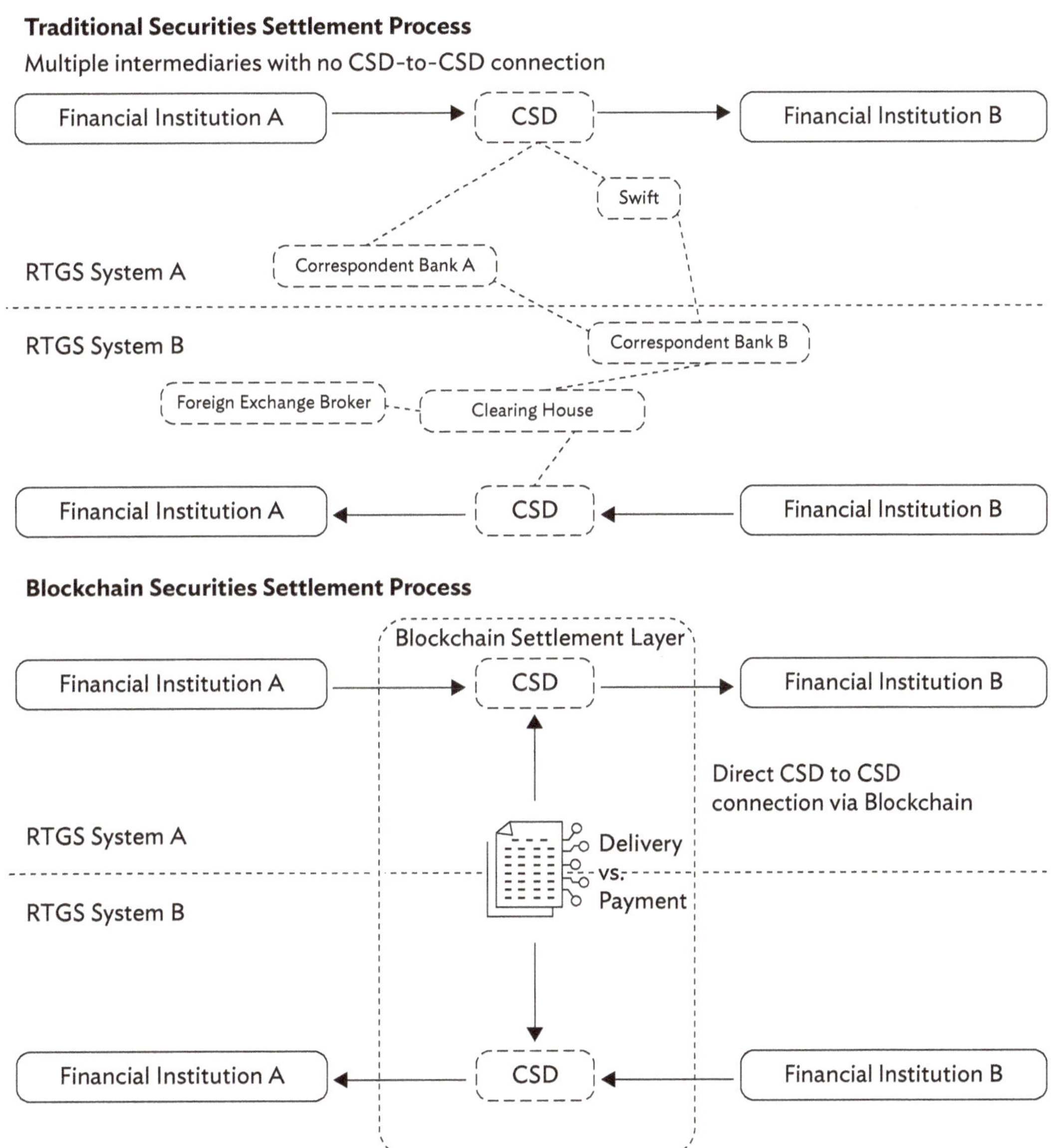

CSD = central securities depository, RTGS = real-time gross settlement.

Note: CSDs can be interlinked via blockchain, enabling domestic or international delivery versus payment settlement flows in real time. This is contrasted with the traditional securities settlement flow which relies upon independent free-of-payment settlement legs via correspondent banks, clearing houses, messaging networks, and foreign exchange brokerages.

Source: Asian Development Bank.

Fujitsu was tasked with connecting the blockchains of the three model economies with its ConnectionChain, which uses the Cacti Ledger Plugin to enable interoperability across the different ledgers.[15] Its extended smart contract function enables it to connect multiple blockchain-based platforms. ConnectionChain also records all transaction processes across the different chains, ensuring transparency.

Given that there were different parties involved in the implementation, the teams conducted regular meetings to align expectations, as well as thresh out issues and identify solutions to these.

Cross-border DVP was executed by dividing the transaction into cross-border and cross-currency payment versus payment, where cash tokens were exchanged, and domestic DVP, where cash and securities tokens were exchanged. This setup was intended to comply with the current regulatory framework wherein currency exchange and fund transfers between two economies are done through a banking system, while securities and cash are exchanged in a domestic payment and settlement system.[16] The simultaneous exchanges of three different tokens was a novel attempt under this initiative; previous POCs only tested two token exchanges. The transaction flow was designed to follow the path of a typical securities settlement in regional markets so that the process could be realistically compared with the existing environment.

ADB specified the entities of each simulated transaction and provided the same instructions in the form of input files to the service providers acting as DVP and payment versus payment facilitators. Some of these instructions deliberately contained nonmatching or missing data to test whether these transaction attempts would be successfully stopped, and the failure was reported. The input files contained either one or multiple instructions, depending on the service provider's preference. The service providers extracted the data from the input files and checked the consistency of information. They then exported the data to their respective blockchains and created ledger entries or transaction records in preparation for the cross-border DVP. Meanwhile, Fujitsu acted as a bridge in the market where the buyer (or seller) was located and made the local currency amount available to a simulated nostro account in the RTGS system of the domestic DVP environment. The service providers acting as the DVP facilitator simulated the minting of an equivalent amount of local currency cash tokens into the account of the buyer's custodian based on the local currency amount funded by Fujitsu. The domestic DVP was carried out once the expected

Table 1: How Blockchain Can Potentially Resolve Cross-Border Transaction Challenges

CHALLENGES	WHAT BLOCKCHAIN OFFERS
• The bilateral host-to-host linkage was costly because it must be linked by a virtual private network. Besides, the linkage may require specifications for each host, which will multiply the costs of the connection as participants in the network increases.	• A blockchain-based platform has the potential to reduce costs of security if it can utilize the open network. Stepwise participation can be accommodated easily as the system is designed to be distributed.
• Current cross-border transaction practices through the correspondent banking network make it very difficult to operationalize the same-day delivery versus payment even in the same time zone.	• A blockchain-based platform enables same-day cross-border delivery versus payment like a host-to-host connection. • A blockchain-based platform can provide an alternative to host-to-host connection.
• The centralized system for regional settlement infrastructure cannot escape from the issue of geopolitical hegemony.	• A blockchain-based platform can decentralize data management with equal status of participating members.

Source: Asian Development Bank.

15 The Cacti Ledger Plugin is part of the Hyperledger Cacti project, an open-source project Fujitsu contributed to. At the time of the POC, the product was called Hyperledger Cactus.

16 In ASEAN+3, central banks and regulators, except Japan, restrict the circulation of currencies and securities outside of their jurisdictions. Therefore, the tokens could be circulated only within the issued jurisdictions. In addition, cash tokens can only be minted by the issuing central bank of the currency, while the security tokens can only be minted by the CSDs where these securities are registered.

amount of local currency cash tokens and security tokens were recorded in the DVP solution and detected and assessed using smart contracts. Fujitsu, once provided with the status update, released the foreign currency.[17] All transactions, including those that failed, were documented through console logs or transaction history files, which were aggregated by Fujitsu in a common journal.

The POC showed that blockchain was workable and fit for purpose for cross-border cross-currency DVP even with the current regulatory environment. Blockchain was seen to be more resilient and tamper-resistant compared to existing payment and settlement systems. The decentralized nature of these platforms reduces the likelihood of data manipulation if properly managed. Thus, a well-designed system that uses blockchain has strong potential to increase efficiency and security. Project Tridecagon showed strong potential for using blockchain for the cross-border cross-currency DVP.

The three different types of blockchain-based platforms—Corda, Ethereum, and Hyperledger Iroha—were successfully connected. The POC proved to be able to execute the simultaneous exchange of three different kinds of tokens, which was the technical highlight of the POC. The processing of cross-border cross-currency DVP transactions (including the blocking of the balance in one economy during cross-border payment versus payment and transferring the money after the transfer was completed in the other economy) was carried out immediately. The "failure" cases (missing or incomplete data) were also successfully handled by the systems.

This is a summary of the results of Project Tridecagon. For the full report, please see ADB. 2023. *Connecting Market Infrastructures in ASEAN+3: The Project Tridecagon Proof of Concept*.

17 The functionality to burn tokens was included in the POC, but it was not used because investors had the option to retain cash or securities tokens in their accounts or wallets instead of converting them.

Blockchain in trade finance. Blockchain can streamline trade finance by digitizing documentation, accelerating processing, and reducing operational risks.

Blockchain for Trade Finance in Thailand and Viet Nam
Improving operational efficiency in trade finance transactions

Highlights

- ADB's Trade Finance Program's end-to-end process is mainly paper-based and manual.
- Blockchain offers various benefits—including operational efficiency, security, and transparency—in the context of trade finance transactions.
- ADB, together with its partners, successfully conducted a live transaction.

Fast Facts

Economies: Thailand, Viet Nam
Years of implementation: 2020
Information Technology Department's partner ADB department: Private Sector Operations Department
ADB partners:
- Contour—technical service provider
- CryptoBLK—technical service provider
- Bank for Investment and Development of Vietnam—issuing bank
- Standard Chartered Bank—confirming bank
- OPEC Plastics Joint Stock Company—importer
- SGC Plastics—exporter

ADB's Trade Finance Program uses the Trade Finance Program Management System and SWIFT to handle the end-to-end trade finance process, including guarantee application and issuance. Trade finance is a paper-heavy industry: various document exchanges take place involving several entities, including exporters, importers, banks, and transportation and logistics companies.[18] Most of the steps involved in the process are manually done.

ADB is a supporter of trade digitalization. Together with the Government of Singapore and the International Chamber of Commerce, it supported the Digital Standards Initiative, which aims to create standards to streamline the interoperability of various digital networks and platforms related to trade. Shifting toward digitalization will not only improve operational efficiency and interoperability, but it will also help establish a system that can be more easily measured, monitored, and regulated.[19] In addition, establishing standards would also help resolve issues with the market of trade finance platforms, which tend to be fragmented, siloed, and not interoperable. As part of its support for digital transformation in the trade sector, ADB sought more efficient ways to process guarantees and loans for trade finance.

[18] S. Wass. 2022. Trade Finance Industry Remains Hopeful on Blockchain Despite Failed Projects. *S&P Global*. 27 October.

[19] ADB. 2022. Global Supply Chains Need Upgrading for a Green, Inclusive, Resilient, and Socially Responsible Future. 22 June.

Blockchain networks can be used to exchange data and documents as digital assets; additionally, these can be further composed with exchanges of value such as duties, fees, and charges. The POC tested whether blockchain could make trade finance transactions quicker while minimizing risk. Standard Chartered Bank and the Bank for Investment and Development of Vietnam were the partner banks for this initiative. Contour, a global network of banks, trade partners, and corporations that used blockchain in its decentralized global trade finance network to enable real-time collaboration among various stakeholders, oversaw the project with ADB.[20] ADB also engaged CryptoBLK to develop additional workflows on the Contour network to enable credit guarantee issuance on behalf of a crediting bank.[21]

The first credit guarantee transaction using blockchain involving $50,000 worth of plastics shipped from Thailand to Viet Nam was successfully conducted in September 2020.[22] This was also the first cross-bank letter of credit transaction that was done using a blockchain-based platform between Thailand and Viet Nam.[23]

The live transaction, which started with Standard Chartered Bank sending its guarantee request and ended with ADB's Trade Finance Program issuing its guarantee issuance, took less than 4.5 hours. In contrast, the standard process could take more than 1 day for the transaction to be completed. Some issues were encountered that caused some delays in the transactions, but the process was still significantly faster compared to the conventional process. ADB also provided feedback to Contour on the areas for improvement, including on the user interface, as well as on the issues that were encountered that were temporarily resolved using workarounds.

The initiative demonstrated that using blockchain in trade finance enabled the faster review and processing of documents compared to the currently used system, thereby increasing efficiency and reducing operational costs. Automation eliminated redundant steps and reduced manual processes. In addition, it offered other benefits, including streamlining processes and enabling real-time tracking of transaction status and an audit trail if needed.

ADB's Trade and Supply Chain Finance Program was keen on scaling up the blockchain-based platform to reach other markets even with no clear assertion from the participating banks to bring the initiative to the next stage of testing. However, Contour put the expansion on hold because it wanted to develop additional capabilities for the platform and make it more robust to support the scale-up. However, Contour was ultimately unable to generate sufficient funding from its bank shareholders, resulting in its closure on 30 November 2023.[24]

20 Contour. Contour: The Trusted Network for Global Trade.

21 Standard Chartered Bank is one of the seven banks that established Contour, alongside Bangkok Bank, CTBC Holding, BNP Paribas, SEB, HSBC, and ING.

22 ADB. ADB Conducts its First Credit Guarantee Using Distributed Ledger Technology for Trade Finance. News release. 11 September.

23 Standard Chartered. 2020. We've completed our first cross-bank Letter of Credit blockchain transaction between Vietnam and Thailand. News release. 11 September.

24 E. Wragg. 2023. Exclusive: Contour to Shut Down as Bank Shareholders Pull Funding. *Global Trade Review*. 27 October.

Figure 4: How Blockchain Can Streamline Trade Processes

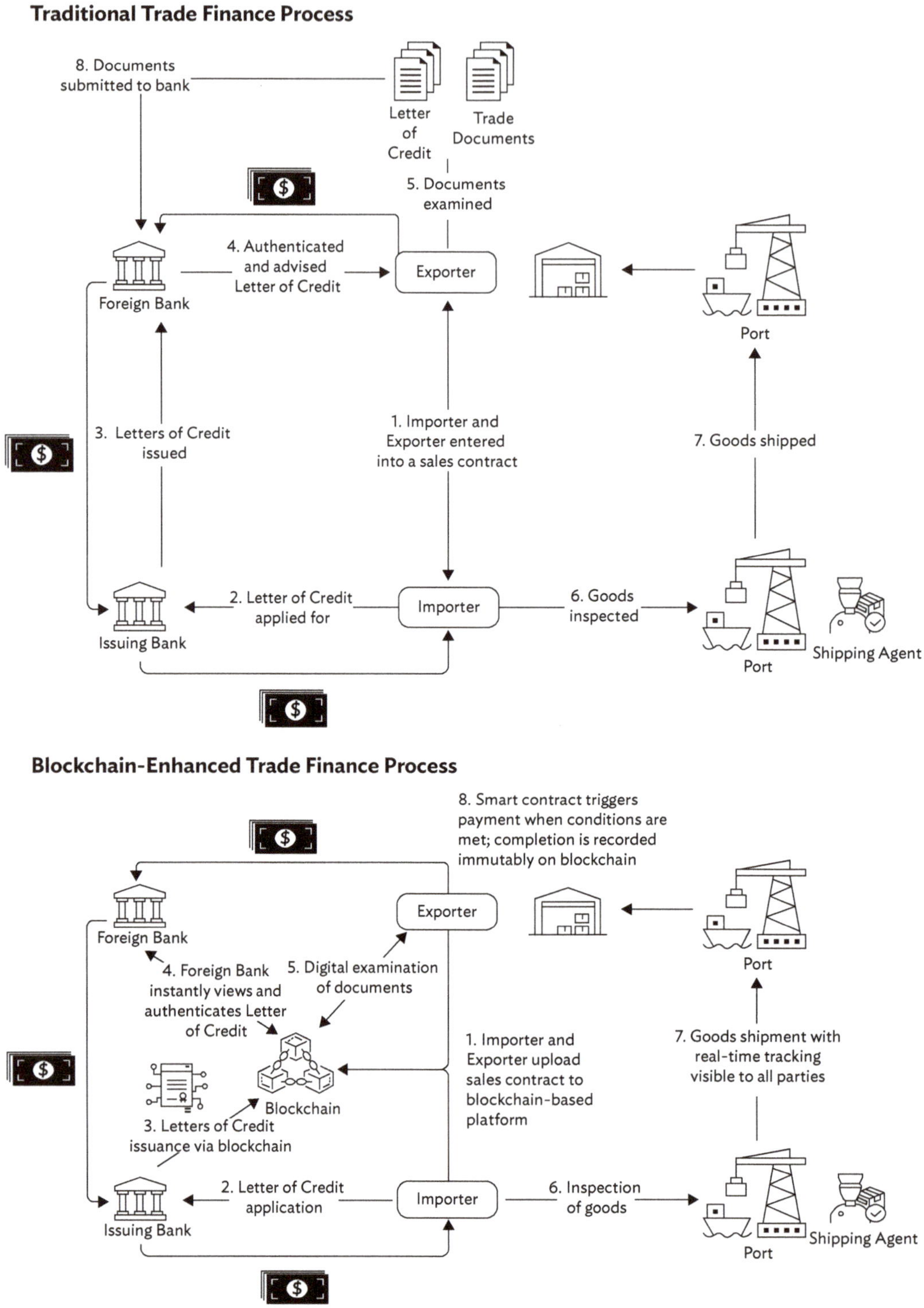

Note: By leveraging blockchain, the exporters and importers could settle trade finance transactions in hours rather than days. Blockchain can also minimize paperwork and enhance transparency mechanisms.

Source: Asian Development Bank.

Blockchain for cross-border data and document sharing. Blockchain can enhance cross-border data and document sharing among multiple stakeholders.

Maldives is one of the smallest countries in Asia and the Pacific. Its economy is heavily reliant on imports, which include essentials such as food and fuel, and exports, primarily of fresh fish and fish products.[25] However, import trade processes in Maldives were constrained by procedural and organizational bottlenecks that forced stakeholders, particularly traders, to shoulder additional costs and losses. In addition, these processes were primarily paper-based, slowing down transactions and making them human resource-intensive. Furthermore, at least some documentary requirements overlapped: physical hard copies had to be submitted to various agencies multiple times. Thus, ADB supported a pilot that tested whether blockchain could be leveraged to improve cross-border data and document sharing chosen from six evaluated options based on strategic impact versus feasibility mapping.[26] Blockchain was selected as the underlying technology owing to its potential of improving supply chain management and addressing the pain points affecting trade in Maldives, as well as contributing to the future operating system of a one-stop electronic platform for trade. It also offered key improvements over traditional technologies, including enhanced privacy, automation of business logic though smart contracts, real-time payments, and improved trust in the trade network.

Blockchain to Supporting Trade Finance in Maldives
Streamlining trade processes with blockchain

Highlights

- Maldives heavily engages in trade, but processes are constrained by procedural and organizational bottlenecks.
- ADB supported the piloting of a blockchain-based platform to address and streamline these processes.
- Constraints in development and budget led to the decision to park the initiative for future consideration.

Fast Facts

Country: Maldives
Start of implementation: 2020
Information Technology Department's partner ADB department: South Asia Department
ADB partners:

- IBM India—technology service provider
- Maldives Ministry of Economic Development and Trade; Maldives Customs Service; Maldives Ports Limited; Bank of Maldives PLC; Maldives Islamic Bank Private Limited; Total Transport Solutions Group; Lily Shipping Private Limited; Asia Forwarding, PLC; State Trading Organization, PLC; Bonito Cargo, Logistics Private Limited—local stakeholders

[25] Development Asia. 2020. How Blockchain Can Improve Supply Chain Transparency in Maldives. 27 April.

[26] ADB. Maldives: South Asia Subregional Economic Cooperation National Single Window Project.

Key stakeholders, including ADB, the project management unit for ADB's South Asia Subregional Economic Cooperation National Single Window Project in Maldives, IBM India, shipping agents, freight forwarders, consignee organizations, customs brokers, Maldives Custom Service, and Maldives Ports Limited, had initial discussions to discuss the requirements. The draft inception report and wireframes were subsequently prepared and approved. The first phase in the development of the platform was done in three sprints, with the platform being built using Hyperledger Fabric 2.0, an open-source blockchain.[27]

The import declaration component was originally supposed to be covered under the third sprint but the development had to be deferred as technical assistance from the United Nations Conference on Trade and Development was needed to develop the application programming interface (API) to integrate the app into ASYCUDAWorld.[28]

Subsequent discussions led to the agreement to proceed with the second phase of the initiative, which ran from August 2021 to the first quarter of 2022. The United Nations Conference on Trade and Development was also engaged during this period to support the development of the APIs.

Various challenges were encountered during the second phase. The stakeholders struggled to reach a consensus on the new scope. In addition, only a partial set of APIs required to integrate the platform into ASYCUDAWorld was delivered and tested because of cost and time constraints. These issues ultimately led to the stakeholders deciding to declare the import declaration component as out of scope. This kept the platform from being production-ready at the end of the pilot and prevented the stakeholders from performing technical and end-to-end testing of APIs.

Nonetheless, stakeholder observations and limited tests were performed to evaluate the platform. These tests included digitally filing arrival notices and bills of lading and understanding how the manifest component could be integrated with legacy systems. Additionally, real-time status updates for port and customs authorities, as well as digital gate pass generation, were also demonstrated. These tests showed that the platform could also improve the user experience because it supported real-time status updates and paperless processing, which made the process smoother across stakeholders. It could support the digital filing of documents such as arrival notices and bills of lading, with updates reflected in real time. In addition, it could generate a digital pass for goods, which was released by the port authority and made available for downloading and printing by all stakeholders in real time. As such, the platform could support faster turnaround time for transactions. The delivery of the manifest component in this initiative also showed that integration with the legacy systems of Maldives Customs Authority and the ports authority was possible with minimal disruption.

Because the end-to-end platform was not realized, the government partners had limited insights on how the platform could be integrated into their system. This, along with the projected high costs for the full development and maintenance of the platform and the updating of the legacy systems to make them blockchain-ready, led to the decision to park this initiative for future consideration.

Lessons of this initiative included ensuring that experts are available and engaged at the onset. Early expert involvement significantly influences technology selection, platform design, implementation feasibility, and long-term sustainability. Thus, early engagement is critical so experts can advise on whether blockchain is the right fit given the challenges being faced and, if so, how it can be integrated effectively to address these issues. In addition, costs across all stages need to be considered. Beyond the development costs, investments also need to be put into maintenance and scale-up, considering that the databases will grow as the volume of transactions rises. There are also corresponding costs in upgrading the existing legacy systems to make them blockchain-ready.

---

27 A wireframe is a basic visual diagram developed to serve as a guide on the layout and structure of a digital product, website, or app. A sprint, meanwhile, is a term used in software development to refer to a defined period identified to complete a specific task.

28 ASYCUDAWorld is the most recent version of the customs management software of the United Nations Conference on Trade and Development's Automated System for Customs Data (ASYCUDA). ASYCUDA. ASYCUDAWorld.

Figure 5: How Blockchain Can Streamline Processing Trade Documents

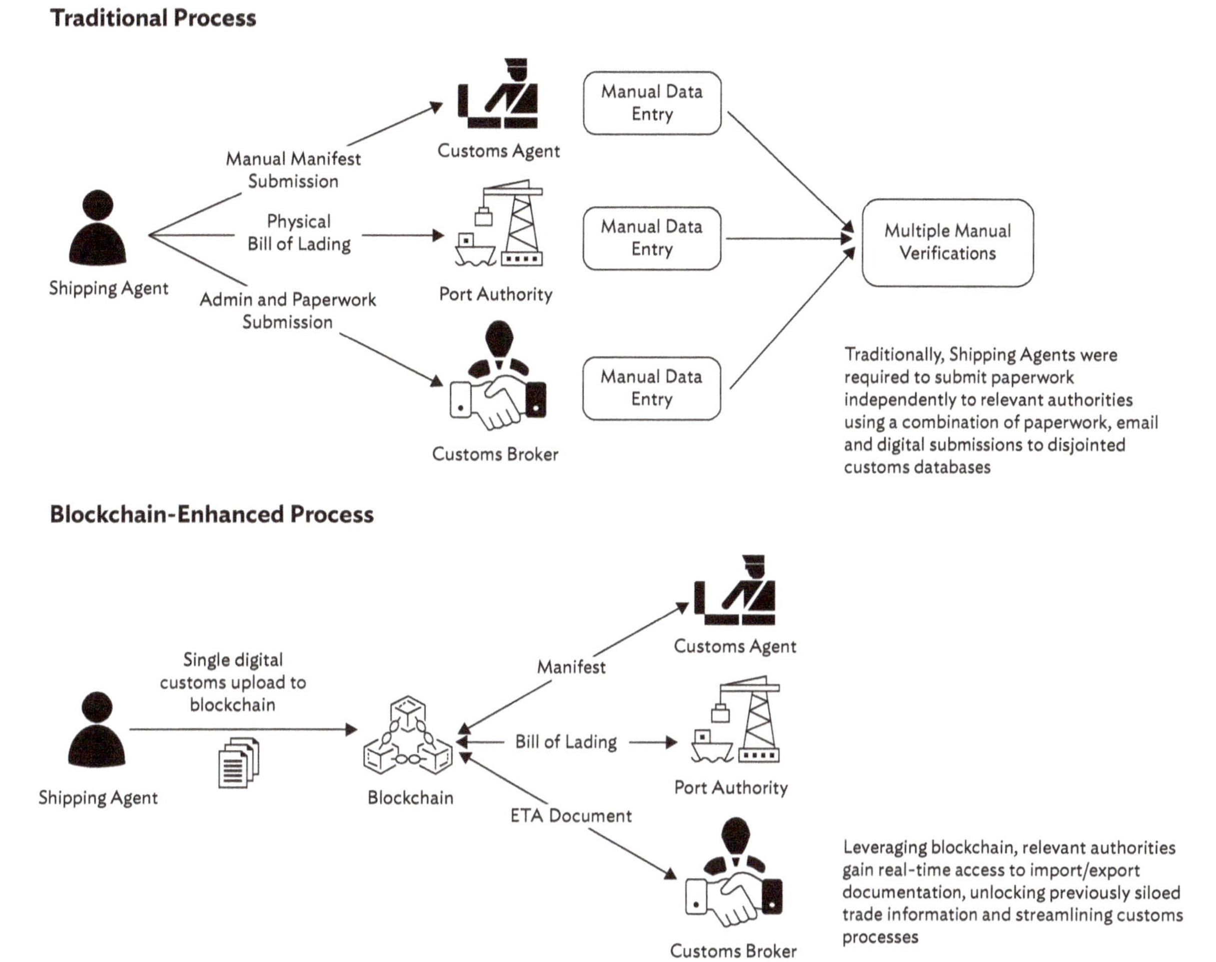

ETA = expected time of arrival.

Note: Blockchain can potentially streamline the processing of trade documents. In addition, enabling a single source of truth minimizes paperwork, un-siloes information, and streamlines customs and operations processes at the port.

Source: Asian Development Bank.

Blockchain and certificates of origin. Blockchain can improve the efficiency of issuing and verifying certificates of origin while reducing risks and costs.

International trade plays a critical economic role in Mongolia, where exports of goods and services made up 69.1% of the gross domestic product as of 2024.[29] The economy showed strong recovery after the pandemic-induced contraction of –4.6% in 2020, achieving 7% gross domestic product growth in 2023.[30]

Efficient trade facilitation has become strategically important to the growth of Mongolia's economy. The country has outlined Vision 2050, which reflects Mongolia's aim to become a "Digital Nation" wherein technology and digital innovations are integrated into all sectors of the economy and society to boost efficiency and production. Thus, the Government of Mongolia has enacted comprehensive legislation to push government digital initiatives to support this vision.

Certificates of origin (COOs) are used to confirm a product's country of origin and serve as the basis for determining what trade rules and tariffs to apply for that specific product.[31] The Mongolia National Chamber of Commerce and Industry (MNCCI) is the authorized entity to issue COOs. The MNCCI issues COOs for the Generalized System of Preferences of 37 countries, 6 countries under the Asia-Pacific Trade Agreement, and the Mongolia-Japan Economic Partnership Agreement. The Mongolian Customs General Administration is responsible for trade compliance and requires that printed COOs are checked against their originals.

Using Blockchain for the Issuance of Certificates of Origin to Boost Mongolian Exports

Promoting security and efficiency in trade using emerging technology

Highlights

- Digitizing certificates of origin (COOs) can open more trade opportunities for Mongolia, where trade is a significant contributor to the economy.
- Blockchain provides a single source of authenticity and immutability.
- ADB supported the development of a minimum viable product (MVP) that uses blockchain to issue and verify online certificates of origin in Mongolia.

Fast Facts

Country: Mongolia
Implementation: April 2023–March 2024
Beneficiaries:

- Mongolia National Chamber of Commerce and Industry
- Customs General Administration Mongolia and Ministry of Foreign Affairs

Information and Technology Department's partner ADB department: East Asia Department
ADB partner: Morpheus Network—technology service provider

29 ADB. Key Indicators Database. Exports of goods and services (% of GDP) (accessed 28 Aug 2025).

30 Mongolia National Chamber of Commerce and Industry. 2024. *Digital Ledger Technology for Certificates of Origin*.

31 International Chamber of Commerce. Certificates of Origin.

Mongolia's full trade potential is constrained by border delays, poor infrastructure, and weak regulatory environment that drive up its trade costs. Various issues affect the ease of verifying the authenticity and accuracy of COOs. The COOs are produced and printed from the MNCCI's database. In cases of inconsistencies or potential fraud, importers, exporters, and border control agencies need to contact the MNCCI to confirm a COO's authenticity, entailing additional costs and delays that defeat the benefits of preferential treatment. This is especially burdensome for the exporters, particularly those who enjoyed low or zero tariffs because of preferential schemes and trade agreements, including free trade agreements.

Trade facilitation and improved utilization of tariff preferences from the Generalized System of Preferences and free trade agreements will help reduce costs to traders, expand exports, and contribute to economic diversification.

Therefore, there was a need to modernize the system not only to make the issuance and verification of COOs more efficient, but also to reduce transaction costs and promote trust and cooperation among trading stakeholders. Doing so would also support the establishment of a national single window facility to further simplify and streamline international trade.[32] Incidentally, this initiative was also supported by ADB through the Regional Improvement of Border Services Project.[33]

The Mongolian Ministry of Foreign Affairs sought ADB's assistance in developing an online portal for verifying COOs. This request came after the Singapore International Chamber of Commerce and Cargo Cloud Pte. Ltd. used blockchain for electronic certificates of origin in 2018.[34] ADB, through its Digital Innovation Sandbox Program, subsequently launched in 2022 a call for submissions for blockchain-based solutions.[35] The firm Morpheus Network was selected to implement the initiative.

This initiative aimed to develop a minimum viable product (MVP) to show whether blockchain could be used to increase efficiency, reduce risk and costs, and streamline the issuance and verification process of COOs. In addition, the MVP should prioritize data security and confidentiality. The intent was to have a platform promoting and maintaining trust and cooperation among trade parties, including chambers of commerce, traders, customs agencies, and other third parties. The result was a self-service portal enabling users to digitally check COOs, where each COO was digitally signed, and where each resulting digital signature was stored on the digital ledger. The ledger is tamper resistant against any unauthorized modification.

The MVP was developed by Morpheus Network based on the Ethereum-compatible public blockchain platform Polygon.

Blockchain has several features that made it a viable choice for addressing the various challenges in relation to COOs. Besides the advantage of greater efficiency with the shift from manual to digital processes, the technology offers immutability of data (or "tamper resistance") as a result of cryptographic hashing and consensus mechanisms built into the network. Blockchain entries, once made, cannot be tampered with as long as the majority of the network participants validate the initial data entry. As such, the digital ledger offers an immutable verification trail to stakeholders to verify accurate and up-to-date information on transactions. This was particularly critical when it came to dealing with COOs, where trust and security are critical to build and maintain international cooperation. The in-built trust and

32 A single window is an electronic facility where parties who are involved in trade and transport can submit standardized information and documents on a single entry point to comply with import, export, and regulatory requirements. United Nations Centre for Trade Facilitation and Electronic Business. 2005. *Recommendation No. 33: Recommendation and Guidelines on Establishing a Single Window*. p. 3.

33 ADB. Mongolia: Regional Improvement of Border Services.

34 Singapore International Chamber of Commerce. 2018. Singapore International Chamber of Commerce and vCargo Cloud Launch World's First Blockchain-based e-Certificate of Origin ("eCO"). News release. 8 May.

35 ADB. ADB Digital Learning Labs Opportunity: Using Blockchain for National Single-window Digital Platform in Mongolia.

immutability of blockchain made it less likely for fraud and errors to occur.[36] Modernizing the system using blockchain also reduced manual administrative processes, resulting in improved operational efficiency and lower compliance costs. Smart contracts were also integrated to further streamline the process of COO issuance and validation. Additional encryption was employed to address the issue of data confidentiality in using a public blockchain, considering that the data involving COOs are confidential.

The firm Morpheus Network was engaged by ADB from April 2023 to March 2024 to design and develop the solution based on the requirements of the working group composed of ADB, the MNCCI, and the Mongolian Customs General Administration.

The project and technical needs assessment was conducted from April to June 2023. This included a review of the existing procedures, legal guidelines, data, and data workflow in the issuance of COOs. Gaps and recommendations were also identified. The Ethereum-compatible public blockchain platform Polygon was subsequently chosen given its technical maturity and cost.

The blockchain-based platform for COOs was developed and delivered from July to November 2023. This included the front-end and back-end features to monitor and verify online the generated digital footprints of COOs.

From December 2023 to March 2024, a set of technical add-ons were identified with the stakeholders, with the main objectives to further consolidate data security and confidentiality, data traceability, monitoring tools (including a blockchain "gas meter"), and improvements of the user interface.

The digital initiative was developed successfully with strong cooperation with the ADB Digital Innovation Sandbox Program and a high level of motivation and participation from the MNCCI.

More than 500 COOs with their digital footprints were processed in real time with neither technical limitations nor errors. Cost analysis demonstrated significant efficiency gains: blockchain transaction costs on Polygon from November 2023 to March 2024 ranged from $0.005 to $0.06 per COO. The cost per transaction using Polygon is lower compared to the fees using Ethereum and Arbitrum, indicating the solution's economically viability as compared with Mongolia's annual COO volume (footnote 30).

The platform was designed to be compatible with the existing system used by the MNCCI while also having the potential to be linked with the enhanced Customs Automated Information System of Mongolia.

The MNCCI expressed its strong interest in expanding its use of blockchain and transforming the MVP into an operational product.[37] There have been discussions to expand the initiative at a national level for the Mongolian Customs General Administration to expand its capacity to process multiple types of certificates (including COOs). Additionally, the portable nature of the MVP demonstrates potential for knowledge sharing across Central Asia Regional Economic Cooperation countries, supporting broader regional digital trade facilitation initiatives.

There is also initial interest in exploring the use of digital technologies to streamline the issuance not only of COOs but also other certificates in other developing member countries and sectors. These include food safety certificates and health certificates.

36 J. Giegling. 2022. In Blockchain We Trust? Certificates of Origin as a Case for Distributed-ledger Technologies. *Journal of Law, Market & innovation*. 1 (1).

37 K. Cromley. 2024. Mongolia Embraces Blockchain for Trade Modernization. *Cointrust*. 23 May.

Figure 6: How Blockchain Can Streamline Processing Certificates of Origin

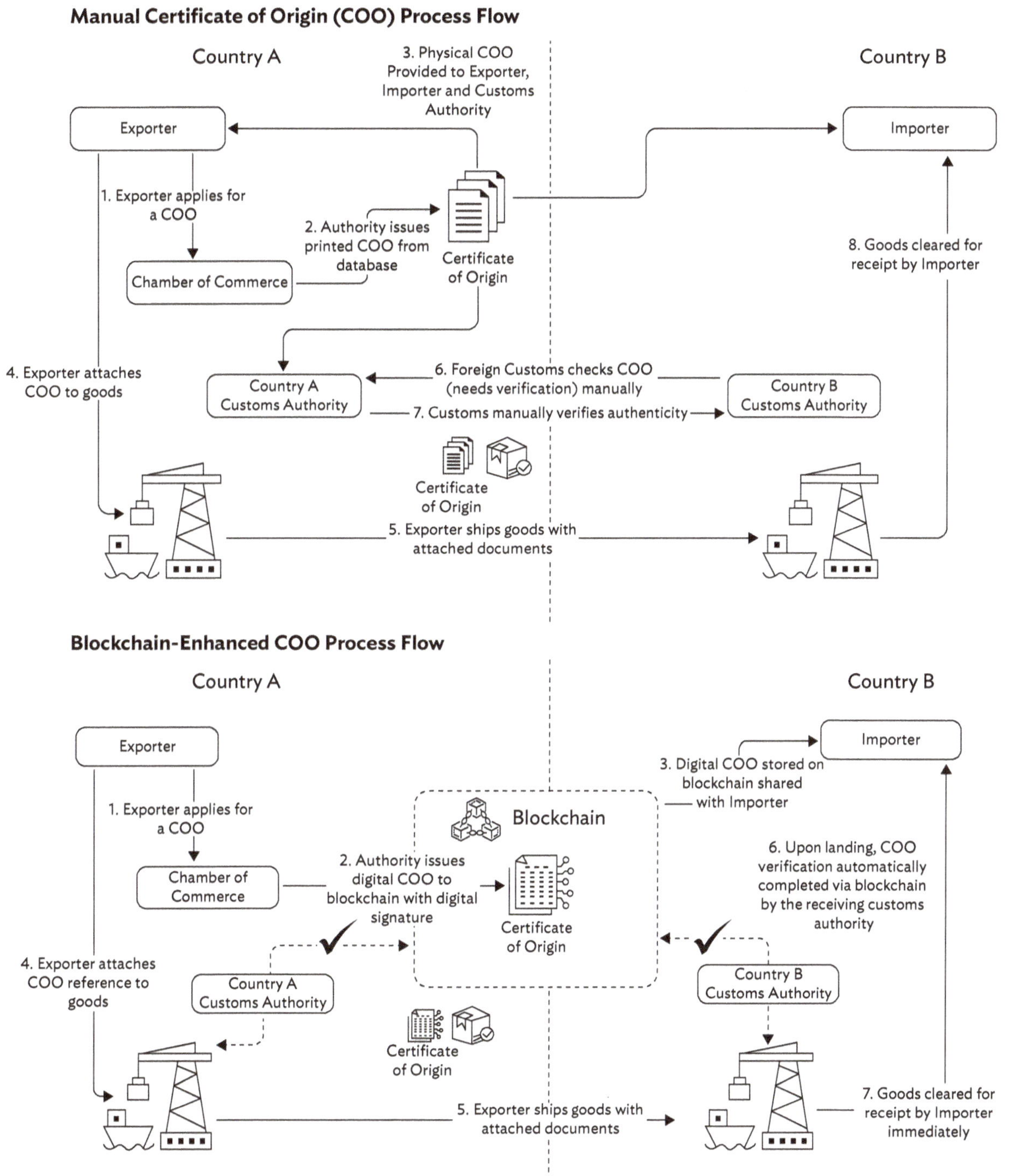

COO = certificate of origin.

Note: In Mongolia, traditionally, stakeholders would be required to contact the Mongolia National Chamber of Commerce and Industry to verify the COOs, and physical paper documents would be required to be attached to goods. With digitization and blockchain, verification can be cut down to minutes because the technology enables near-instant verification by stakeholders in the importation and exportation supply chain.

Source: Asian Development Bank.

Figure 7: Sample Interfaces of the Blockchain-Powered Platform for Certificates of Origin in Mongolia

Note: These are screenshots of the minimum viable product of the blockchain-powered platform for certificates of origin.

Source: Asian Development Bank.

Blockchain and the environment. Blockchain can support climate action by improving transparency, traceability, and trust in carbon markets and by supporting fundraising efforts.

CHAPTER 3
Blockchain for Climate Change Adaptation and Environmental Protection

Blockchain can be used to facilitate innovative approaches to fundraising and carbon trading. By enabling secure, transparent, and traceable digital transactions, it can help overcome barriers like fragmented data, limited market access, and donor engagement. However, its impact will depend on project design, strong partnerships, and alignment with local contexts.

Blockchain for carbon trading. Blockchain can be leveraged to create a shared master ledger that promotes greater transparency in carbon markets.

Testing Blockchain on the Carbon Trading Marketplace in Shanghai, People's Republic of China
Trialing a blockchain-based carbon trading platform

Highlights

- The People's Republic of China (PRC) has been the world's largest emitter of carbon dioxide since 2006.
- The PRC decided to implement a national emission trading scheme in 2017 to limit and reduce carbon dioxide emissions in a cost-effective manner.
- A blockchain-based platform was developed and tested to see if it could address the existing issues related to carbon trading.

Fast Facts

Year of implementation: 2021
Information Technology Department's partner ADB department: East Asia Department
ADB partners:

- Shanghai Environment and Energy Exchange—ADB's implementation partner and POC sponsor
- Zhongchao Blockchain Technology Research Institute—technology service provider
- Timing Carbon Asset Management Co. Ltd.—business consultancy services

Since 2006, the People's Republic of China (PRC) has been the world's largest emitter of carbon dioxide annually.[38] This mainly stems from coal, including coal-fired power stations, coal mining, and blast furnaces producing iron and steel.[39] The PRC's greenhouse gas emissions reached 14,093 million metric tons of carbon dioxide in 2019, passing the 14-gigaton threshold for the first time. This is more than triple its 1990 emissions and a 25% increase in 2009. The PRC alone contributed to more than 27% of the 52-gigaton global emissions in 2019. It also surpassed the combined emissions of all developed countries for the first time.[40]

In 2017, the PRC decided to implement a national emission trading scheme to limit and reduce carbon dioxide emissions in a cost-effective manner. ADB provided technical assistance in designing the national emission trading scheme.[41]

The national emission trading scheme became operational in 2021, with its scope including annual emissions close to 4.5 billion tons of carbon dioxide per year, or about 40% of the PRC's total emissions, mostly carbon, from the power industry. The national emission trading scheme obligated more than 2,000 big emitters in the power sector to account for their 2019 and 2020 emissions.

38 H. Regan and C. Dotto. 2021. US vs. China: How the World's Two Biggest Emitters Stack Up on Climate. *CNN*. 3 November.

39 J. Ambrose. 2019. Methane emissions from coalmines could stoke climate crisis – study. *The Guardian*. 15 November; and L. Myllyvirta. 2021. Analysis: China's carbon emissions grow at fastest rate for more than a decade. *Carbon Brief*. 20 May.

40 *Rhodium Group*. 2021. China's Greenhouse Gas Emissions Exceeded the Developed World for the First Time in 2019. 6 May.

41 ADB. 2018. *Technical Assistance to the People's Republic of China for Improving the Design of the National Carbon Emissions Trading System*.

Carbon assets trading commenced on the platform operated by the Shanghai Environment and Energy Exchange in July 2021. However, the carbon market infrastructure faced some challenges:

(i) **Double counting of carbon credits.** The registries and exchanges maintained manual records in silos. There was no master ledger to verify the entries in real time.

(ii) **Issues with manual verification.** Carbon emission tracking and verification was done manually, which was time and labor-intensive, as well as prone to erroneous recordkeeping.

(iii) **Information asymmetry in carbon markets.** The carbon markets were scattered, worked in silos, and were characterized by information asymmetry, making it difficult for regulators to efficiently supervise carbon issuances for every project application per registry and monitor trading per exchange. The disconnect between Verified Carbon Standard Registry providers increases cost and friction on the carbon credit secondary markets.

The Shanghai Environment and Energy Exchange collaborated with ADB's Digital Innovation Sandbox, which provides a safe and neutral environment for ADB to pilot innovative and relevant emerging technology solutions, to develop and test a solution to address these challenges. The Zhongchao Blockchain Technology Research Institute was engaged as the technology service provider, while Timing Carbon Asset Management Co. Ltd. provided business consultancy services.

The result was a blockchain-based platform that served as a master database and acted as a single source of truth on carbon assets and credit issuance. All relevant transactions and data related to the carbon units on the ledger, including their origin and ownership, could be tracked by potential buyers in real time, enhancing transparency and verifiability of records to address issues on double counting and duplicate trading of carbon assets. Automation improved efficiency and lowered associated costs while reducing the likelihood of errors. The technology did not require end users to be on the blockchain to trade verified carbon units; instead, their point of contact was the web application.

While the test showed the viability of using blockchain in carbon trading, its use does not exist in a vacuum. There are compliance and regulatory gaps related to international carbon trading that need to be addressed should this initiative be scaled up and rolled out in the future.

Figure 8: How Blockchain Can Serve as a Master Database in Carbon Trading

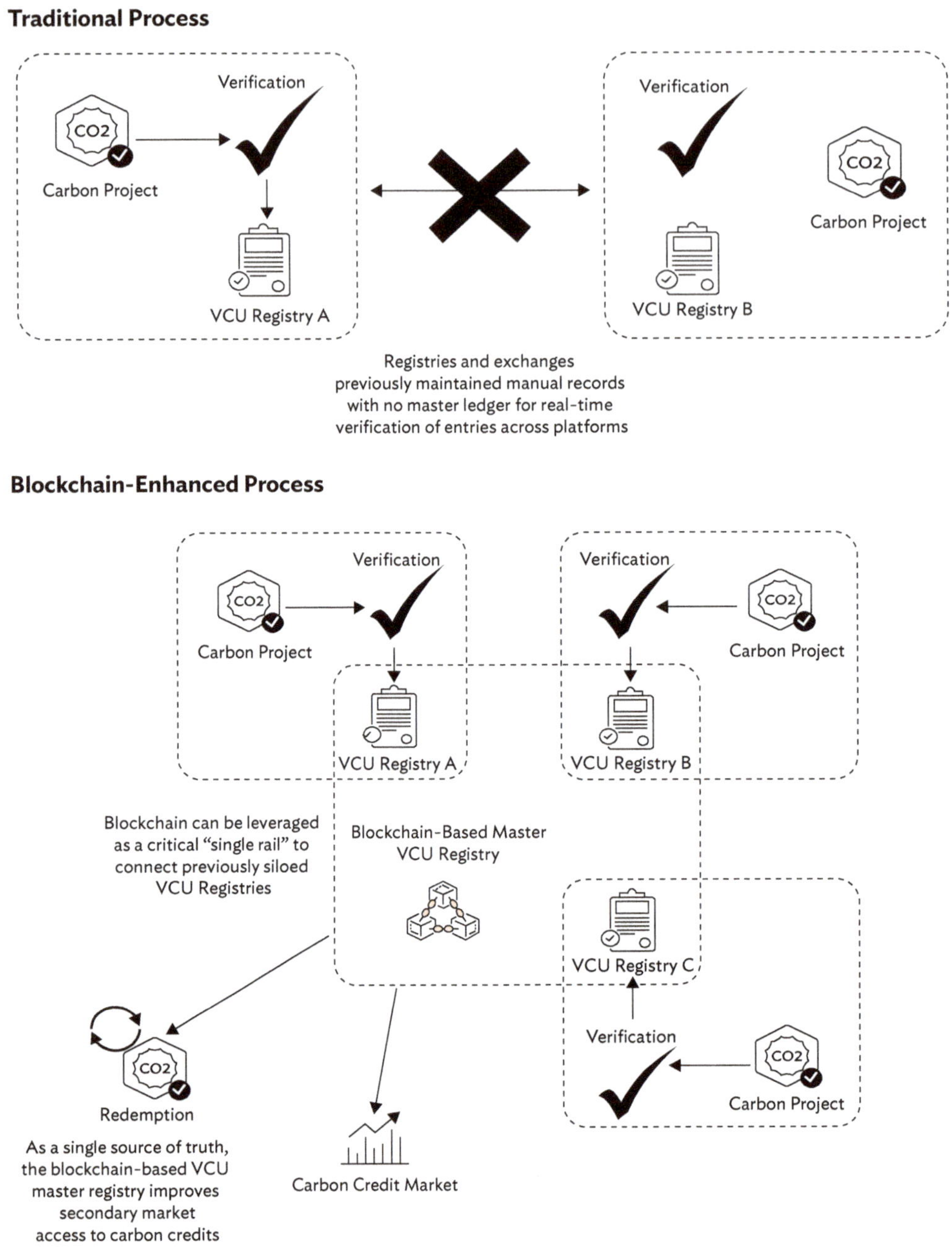

VCU = Verified Carbon Unit.

Note: Blockchain offers a streamlined approach to carbon credit market infrastructure and broke down silos between competing Verified Carbon Standard registry systems. Leveraging it can efficiently connect carbon credit originators with a secondary market, with enhanced transparency, and with reduced costs and settlement times. Connecting these entities cuts down settlement costs and times.

Source: Asian Development Bank.

Blockchain and carbon markets. Blockchain can streamline carbon credit issuance and expand access to international markets.

As the first carbon-negative country in the world, Bhutan has a strong potential for carbon credits.[42] It sequesters more carbon than it emits, producing less than 4 million tons while absorbing more than 9 million tons, thanks largely to its forests.[43] Also contributing to its low carbon emissions is its reliance on renewable energy for electricity. Only about 6% of the country's potential hydropower capacity has been tapped, but it is already generating surplus power, which the country exports to India. These power exports significantly contribute to Bhutan's total gross domestic product.[44] Bhutan also has the potential to exploit other renewable energy sources, including solar, wind, and bioenergy, providing it with additional means to generate carbon credits.[45]

Bhutan, however, faced various challenges in entering the carbon market. Carbon credit issuance was time-consuming and expensive: the end-to-end process could take from 1 to 2 years and cost $200,000–$300,000. The high cost was primarily because of the paper-based and manual processing of transactions: issuing one carbon credit involved auditors, brokers, professional services firms, and national agencies. In addition, Bhutan has limited access to international markets. It engages brokers to find buyers, adding to the already high costs.

Testing Blockchain in Bhutan's Carbon Trading Marketplace
Exploring blockchain's potential in supporting carbon reduction and trading

Highlights

- Bhutan has strong potential for selling carbon credits but faces various challenges in entering the market.
- Blockchain's key features—automated trust, and being transparent, secure, efficient, and auditable—can help address issues with the carbon market.
- A new testing phase is being proposed to cover the launching of a national carbon credit aggregation platform.

Fast Facts

Country: Bhutan
Years of implementation: 2021–2022
Information Technology Department's partner
ADB department: South Asia Department
ADB partners:

- Druk Holdings and Investments—commercial and investment arm of the Government of Bhutan
- InfraBlocks Technologies Pte. Ltd.—technology service provider

[42] Climate Council. 2017. Bhutan is the World's Only Carbon Negative Country, So How Did They Do It? 2 April.

[43] L. Goering. 2021. Forget Net-zero: Meet the Small-nation, Carbon-negative Club. *Reuters*. 4 November.

[44] South Asia Regional Initiative for Energy Integration. 2016. *Working Paper: Impact of Cross-Border Electricity Trade on Bhutan (Country Series)*.

[45] International Renewable Energy Agency. 2019. Renewables in the Kingdom of Bhutan: Supporting the Pursuit of Happiness. 16 December.

These issues were compounded by other challenges in carbon trading. The carbon markets were scattered in silos, making it difficult for regulators to efficiently supervise carbon credit issuance per registry and monitor trading per exchange. This issue also made recordkeeping prone to error and double counting.[46] The lack of a master ledger that recorded all carbon market transactions made it difficult to determine whether the same carbon credits were repeatedly resold. Carbon credits also differed in quality. As such, buyers were uncertain whether the purchased credits would be sufficient to offset actual carbon emissions.[47]

Bhutan, through Druk Holding and Investments, which is fully owned by the Government of Bhutan, sought to develop a digitized national carbon credit issuance portal for the registration and trading of carbon credits with the support of ADB. The first phase saw the development of a POC, which included a comprehensive report on Bhutan's hydropower capacity, the components and limitations of blockchain for carbon markets, and the technical requirements and process to produce an MVP. The second phase covered the MVP development, utilizing the Ethereum network as hosting infrastructure. It focused on the Dagacchu

Figure 9: How Blockchain Can Streamline the Issuance of Carbon Credits

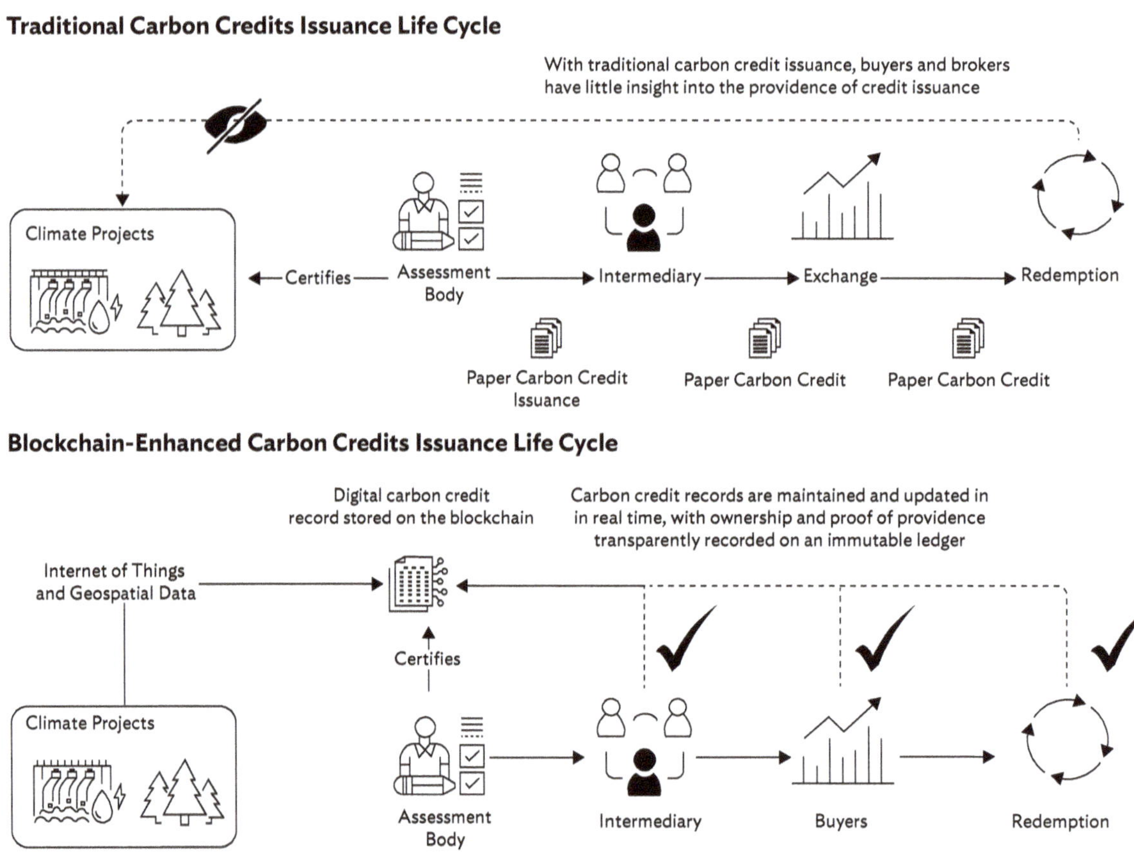

Note: Introducing blockchain alongside technologies such as Internet of Things for carbon credit monitoring and issuance offers the potential to streamline credit issuance opportunities, minimize trust, and enable greater access to international carbon credit markets.

Source: Asian Development Bank.

[46] United Nations Development Programme. 2022. What Are Carbon Markets and Why Are They Important? 18 May.

[47] A. Sahay, S. Hughes, and J. Henretig. 2022. Beyond the Buzz: What Can Blockchain Do for Carbon Markets? *RMI*. 11 November.

hydropower project, an existing carbon credit project in Bhutan.

The MVP had the following modules:

(i) **Real-time carbon data gathering.** The carbon platform collects data, which will serve as the basis for carbon credit metrics.
(ii) **Automated greenhouse gas calculation and data analysis module.** The platform comes with a tool to calculate greenhouse gas reductions following international carbon standards.
(iii) **Carbon credit issuance and verification module.** The platform enables seamless carbon credit issuance and verification, which are also aligned with international carbon standards.
(iv) **Collaboration module.** The platform enables collaboration between internal and external teams, including auditors.

Several mechanisms were also put in place to ensure that "proof of origin" of data can be verified to safeguard the integrity of the carbon credits.

A third phase of the testing was proposed to cover the development of a minimum marketable product and the launching of a national carbon credit aggregation platform, which will serve as a marketplace with access to international markets. The proposal aimed to test whether the platform could be used to make a live transaction, as well as assess what other assets of Bhutan have the potential for generating nature-based credits.

Table 2: Issues with Carbon Credit Trading and How Blockchain Can Potentially Address These

CHALLENGES	BLOCKCHAIN SOLUTION IMPROVEMENTS
Time and cost. Carbon credits have a 1–2 year processing lead time, with costs up to \$200,000–\$300,000 per issuance. Additionally, issuance has a complex life cycle with multiple intermediaries.	With blockchain, carbon credits can be processed in near real time with minimal operating costs via smart contracts.
Trust and data quality. Traditional carbon credit issuance has uncertain data quality; for example, it is prone to miscalculation or double counting. Additionally, there exists no unified verification for carbon credit issuance. All issuance is documented via paper-based records, fragmenting access to information for important stakeholders such as regulators and brokers.	Blockchains can be used to verify proof of origin for carbon credits. Credit proof is stored on an immutable ledger where compliance can be standardized. These are collected in real time, stored digitally, and can be cryptographically authenticated.
Market access. Market access is restricted in traditional issuance, and is typically limited to regional buyers and dependent on brokers. There is no direct access to markets.	A digital platform offered Bhutan a global reach, allowing for direct connections between buyers and sellers of carbon credits and near-instant trading capabilities.

Source: Asian Development Bank.

Nonfungible tokens and fundraising. Nonfungible tokens can support innovative approaches to standard processes, including fundraising.

Non-fungible tokens (NFTs) are digital tokens that represent unique assets, including images, videos, and audio files. Each NFT is unique and not interchangeable even if two or more look alike because each one contains information specific to the asset it represents.

The rising interest in NFTs led ADB to open the "NFTs for Development in Asia" challenge in 2021 to explore opportunities in which these could potentially be used to advance ADB's Strategy 2030 operational priorities. Out of 99 teams that participated in the challenge, Fauna Conservation NFT's proposal to use NFTs for conservation funding was selected by ADB to proceed with implementation.

Fauna Conservation NFT sought to demonstrate that NFTs could be used as a novel fundraising mechanism to support conservation efforts. The intent was to leverage new technology to engage new donors and complement conventional fundraising approaches.

An NFT is created through a process called minting, wherein key information specific to the asset is encrypted and recorded on a new block in a chain using digital ledger technology. These NFTs are

Non-Fungible Tokens for Development in Indonesia
Trialing non-fungible tokens as a fundraising tool

Highlights

- ADB opened a call for proposals on how non-fungible tokens (NFTs) could be used to advance ADB's Strategy 2030.
- Fauna Conservation NFT, the selected team, sought to demonstrate the potential of NFTs in fundraising.
- Despite missing targets, the initiative demonstrated that NFTs have the potential to be leveraged for fundraising.

Fast Facts

Country: Indonesia
Start of implementation: 2021
ADB partners:
- Fauna Conservation NFT—technology service provider
- Indonesian Climate Change Trust Fund—Indonesian government agency partner
- Reef Check Indonesia—Indonesian nongovernment organization partner

available for purchase on online platforms, thereby allowing an international market to buy and sell NFTs using cryptocurrency. Smart contracts are used for NFT sales, making every purchase traceable and immutable and ensuring secure transactions.[48] NFTs also offer efficiency: transactions involving digital assets can be done quickly and easily for users' convenience.

Fauna Conservation NFT aimed to leverage the indivisible and nonreplicable nature of NFTs that makes them collectible. Their team sought to use gamification to encourage people to buy and sell NFTs in support of a conservation cause.

The Coral Reef Rehabilitation and Management Program—Coral Triangle Initiative Project, which was supported in Indonesia by ADB and the Indonesian Climate Change Trust Fund, was identified as the project where the initiative would be tested. Reef Check Indonesia, a nongovernment organization that was involved in the project, agreed to be the implementation partner. Impact Hub Manila, which provided management support, in coordination with ADB's Information Technology Department, also searched for experts to mentor Fauna Conservation NFT throughout the process.

Fauna Conservation NFT, with the support of a mentor and in coordination with Reef Check Indonesia, identified the animals that were featured in the NFT collection. Fauna Conservation NFT opted to render the designs in 3D to make them look realistic and stand out from the conventional 2D images of other NFTs. It also engaged an artist from a Cambodia-based design studio to create the artwork for the collection.

The "Non-Fungible Reef" NFT collection featured four unique animal designs: the giant manta ray (*Mobula birostris*), peacock mantis shrimp (*Odontodactylus scyllarus*), raccoon butterflyfish (*Chaetodon lunula*), and common octopus (*Octopus vulgaris*). Three designs were launched on 4 December 2022 and the fourth on 26 May 2023. A total of 380 NFTs based on these four designs were created (150 raccoon butterfly fish, 100 giant manta ray, 50 peacock mantis shrimp, 50 common octopus). The collection was launched on OpenSea, the world's largest online NFT marketplace.

Social media channels were used to promote the sales of the NFTs and to raise conservation awareness.

Figure 10: How Non-Fungible Tokens Can Be Leveraged for Fundraising

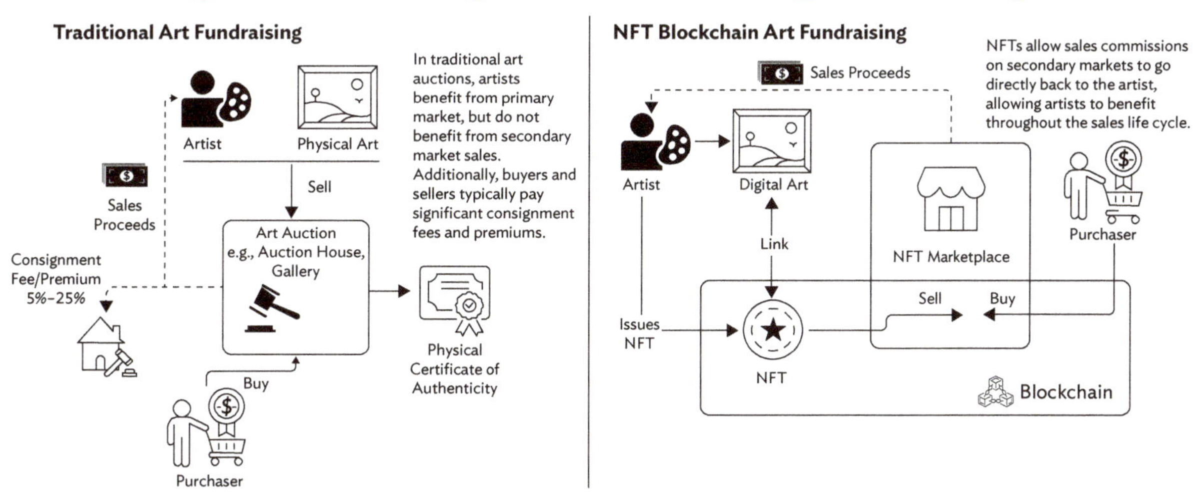

NFT = non-fungible token.

Note: In traditional art fundraising, artists typically partner with a gallery, broker, or auction house, limiting their market reach. Artists only benefit from the first sale and often pay hefty commissions or consignment fees on sale. Leveraging NFTs for the sale of art and media, artists and fundraisers can access a global audience, experiment with a new digital medium, and collect proceeds from the sale of artwork throughout the secondary market life cycle via on-chain commissions.

Source: Asian Development Bank.

48 R. Sharma. 2024. Non-Fungible Token (NFT): What It Means and How It Works. *Investopedia*. 12 June.

Some delays were encountered in developing the NFTs, resulting in the collection being released during the cryptocurrency market crash in 2022, which continued until 2023. The NFTs were priced lower than the original plan of Fauna Conservation NFT to try to compensate for this.

The following were the number of NFTs sold per design: 15 of the giant manta ray, 17 of the peacock mantis shrimp, 22 of the raccoon butterflyfish, and 3 of the common octopus. Payments were made in cryptocurrency. Sales reached DAI 366 and ETH 0.7, equivalent to $2,653.16 as of April 2024. Ownership of the unsold NFTs, along with the sales proceeds, was transferred to Reef Check Indonesia at the end of implementation.

Blockchain and rights protection. By enabling secure, transparent, and interoperable records, blockchain can help strengthen human and land rights.

CHAPTER 4

Blockchain for the Promotion of Human and Land Rights

Blockchain holds the potential for being used as a tool to help protect human and land rights. ADB has piloted two cases in areas that are critical to inclusive development: land rights and educational credentials. These initiatives show the potential of blockchain in supporting more equitable access to resources and opportunities, reducing fraud, and improving interoperability between stakeholders, laying the groundwork for more resilient and inclusive digital ecosystems.

Blockchain in land management. Blockchain can support secure recordkeeping, faster approvals, and improved transparency, contributing to enhanced efficiency in land administration.

Developing a Blockchain-Based Digital Platform to Transform the Customary Land Leasing Process in Fiji
Developing a tamper-proof land leasing digital platform for iTaukei lands in Fiji

Highlights

- The Government of Fiji sought to undergo digital transformation.
- ADB previously supported the digital transformation of the iTaukei Land Trust Board (TLTB), including the development of a blockchain-based digital platform for its land registry.
- The TLTB sought additional assistance from ADB to integrate the Land Development Vetting Committee portal into the blockchain-based platform, as well as develop a POC of a landowners' portal.

Fast Facts

Country: Fiji
Year of implementation: 2023
Information and Technology Department's partner
ADB department: Pacific Department
ADB partners:
- TLTB
- Land Development Vetting Committee, comprising the TLTB, the Ministry of Lands, and the Department of Town and Country Planning
- KPMG Digital Village—technical service provider

In 2012, the Government of Fiji launched the Digital Government Transformation Programme, otherwise known as digitalFIJI, which aimed to improve the quality and accessibility of government services using digital tools.[49] One of the aims of digitalFIJI was to improve internal processes and efficiency, as well as streamline service delivery.

The land leasing system in Fiji stood to benefit from digitalization. About 90% of land in Fiji is owned by indigenous Fijians. Called iTaukei land, it can neither be bought nor sold except to the state for a public purpose. However, it can be leased to investors. The iTaukei Land Trust Board (TLTB) is the government agency responsible for administering, developing, and managing lands in Fiji on behalf of their owners, as stipulated in the Native Land Trust Board Act, 1940.[50] Landowners must consent to have the land leased before the TLTB can issue the binding leases or agreements.

Back in 2017, the land leasing process was largely manual and paper-based, which carried its own set of risks. Data loss was a risk in the event of natural or manufactured events. Fiji is particularly vulnerable to sea level rise and flooding because of climate change.[51] In addition, there have been reports of fire incidences in the TLTB's premises, further driving home the risks of relying on paper-based documentation. Besides the issue of data loss, the cumbersome process and various paperwork required

49 Government of Fiji. Digital Government Transformation.

50 iTaukei Land Trust Board. Corporate Information.

51 ADB. 2013. Fiji's Losses from Climate Change Could Reach 4% of GDP by 2100. News release. 26 November.

in land leasing meant that processing documents could take as long as 2 to 3 years and required investors to visit the TLTB offices several times. Tracking the bottlenecks was difficult because the government agencies involved in land leasing worked independently.

ADB provided 4-year technical assistance to the TLTB for the test demonstration of a land price index based on historical lease transactions under the Promoting Smart Systems in ADB's Future Cities Program.[52] This also covered the initial digitization of land leasing documents handled by the TLTB.

Figure 11: How Blockchain Can Be Leveraged in the Land Registry Process

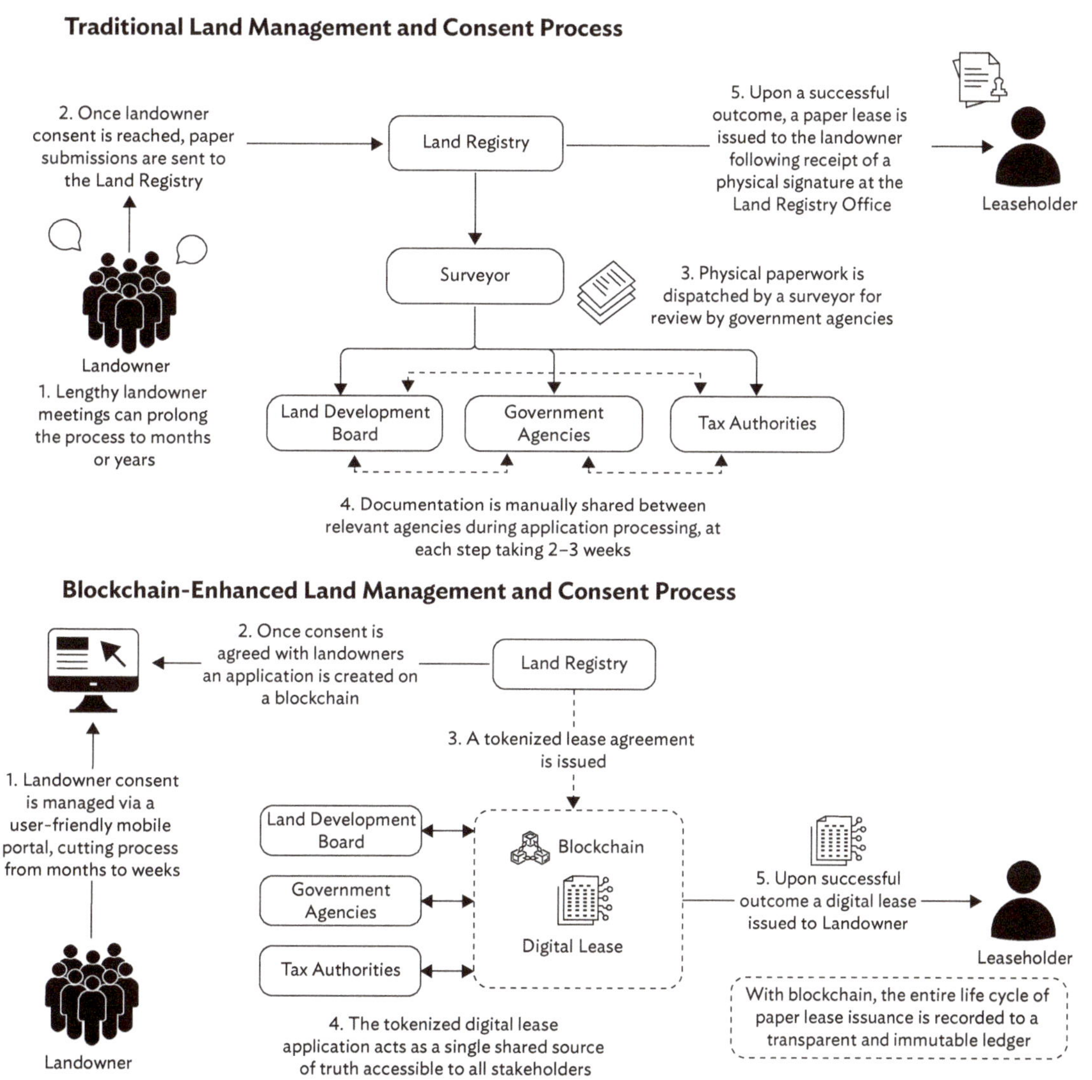

Note: Leveraging blockchain can potentially reduce processing time from 2 to 3 years to months or even weeks by replacing paper-based workflows with integrated digital processes. It can connect previously siloed government agencies to a shared blockchain platform, enabling real-time data sharing, mobile landowner consent, and disaster-resistant record storage. Doing so limits multiple office visits, reduces data loss risks, and improves transparency for all stakeholders—landowners, investors, and government agencies.

Source: Asian Development Bank.

[52] ADB. Regional: Promoting Smart Systems in ADB's Future Cities Program.

Additional financing from the High-Level Technology Fund extended the technical assistance until 2020, which supported the development of a prototype, and later an MVP, of a digital platform that used blockchain, as well as user acceptance testing among the TLTB's stakeholders. The digital platform cocreated by the TLTB, ADB, and KPMG Digital Village was officially launched by the Government of Fiji in 2022.

The TLTB deemed that blockchain was the appropriate solution to address the specific challenge of land leasing. Subsequently, the agency championed using the blockchain-based platform to other government agencies in Fiji. It also approached ADB to get additional technical assistance to enhance the blockchain-based land leasing platform to include several portals and systems used by other relevant government agencies to harmonize data and approvals. These portals were in silos and not interoperable, making data sharing difficult. These also needed to be made scalable given the large volumes of documents they were and will be handling.

KPMG Digital Village, which codeveloped the TLTB's blockchain-based platform with ADB, was again engaged to do the enhancements. The TLTB assisted ADB in coordinating with the other government agencies whose portals will be included in the platform integration. The team also consulted with landowners from differing backgrounds to get their insights to support the development of the landowner portal. A POC was later developed to include a mobile voting feature that would allow landowners to provide their consent digitally on the de-reservation of their customary land to make it available for lease. The POC was designed to give the TLTB the option to adopt this landowner portal, which would help further speed up the land leasing process.

The 5-month reengagement with the Information Technology Department's Digital Innovation Sandbox Program saw the successful integration of the TLTB's existing Land Development Vetting Committee portal into the ADB-supported blockchain-based land leasing platform. This was launched in mid-2023.

Capacity building was provided to key Government of Fiji officials and personnel to enable them to continue integrating other agencies into the blockchain platform should they wish to do so.

Figure 12: Screenshot of the iTaukei Online Marketplace Showing Lands Available for Lease

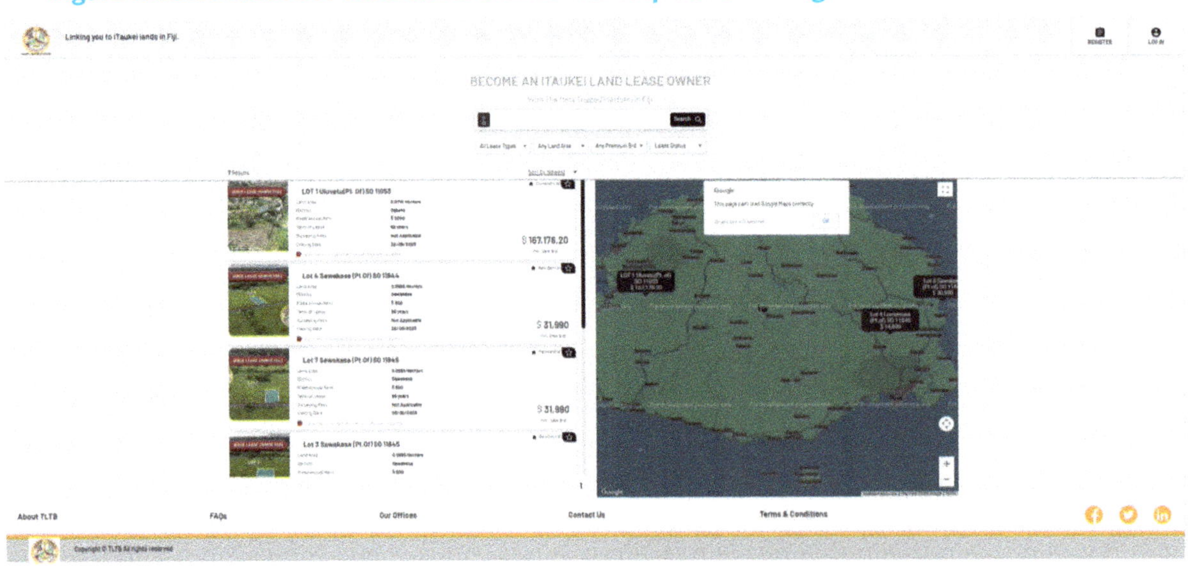

Source: iTaukei Land Trust Board. Become an iTaukei Land Lease Owner.

Blockchain and education. One potential use case of blockchain in education is the issuance and verification of academic credentials.

When the coronavirus disease (COVID-19) pandemic forced universities worldwide into emergency remote learning, Indonesia saw an opportunity to revolutionize higher education with blockchain. This was also the time when massive open online courses became widely available.

Indonesia is one of the countries with the most progressive regulatory frameworks for credit transfers.[53] The Indonesian Cyber Education (ICE) Institute was established by the Government of Indonesia as a marketplace of online courses where students can learn, even at the height of the restrictions brought by the COVID-19 pandemic. Operated by Universitas Terbuka, the ICE Institute was established to advance online education in Indonesia by curating all online courses, whether Indonesian or international, and overseeing the quality of these offerings.[54] Therefore, the ICE Institute is responsible for big data not only in relation to the online course offerings it manages, but also students' records.

The ICE Institute's vision is to have a sustainable and competitive advantage. Its establishment is aligned with the Ministry of Research and Technology and Higher Education Regulation No. 51 of 2018 and

Blockchain for Digital Credentialing in Indonesia
Testing blockchain's potential to support online learning in Indonesia

Highlights

- The coronavirus disease (COVID-19) pandemic led to a spike in demand for massive open online courses, which allow learners to learn anytime and anywhere.
- The Indonesian Cyber Education (ICE) Institute is a marketplace for quality-assured higher education courses offered by local and international universities.
- ADB supported the ICE Institute in leveraging blockchain to resolve trust and traceability issues involving digital credentials.

Fast Facts

Country: Indonesia
Years of implementation: 2020–2021
Information Technology Department's partner
ADB department: Southeast Asia Department
ADB partner: ICE Institute

[53] M. Garcia, L. D. Perez, and R. Hayashi. 2021. Accreditation of Online Courses in Higher Education—Early Adopters in the European Union, India, Indonesia, and Malaysia. *ADB Briefs*. No. 196. November. ADB.

[54] P. Pannen. 2021. Quality Assurance in Online Learning at Scale at the Indonesia Cyber Education Institute. In S. Ra, S. Jagganathan, and R. Maclean, eds. *Powering a Learning Society During an Age of Disruption*. ADB and Springer. pp. 121–134.

the Ministry of Education and Culture Regulation No. 7 of 2020. Through the ICE Institute, students can earn credits online, which can be stacked or aggregated to form up to 40% of the study program, 50% of which can be obtained outside of the higher education institution where the student is enrolled (footnote 54).

Since its inception, the ICE Institute has identified the use of blockchain for its digital credentialing system as a tool to help address trust and traceability issues.

Immutability and transparency offered by blockchain could help lessen or eliminate the proliferation of fake diplomas and diploma mills, as the quality of the credentials would be assured, even in cases of course and credit transfers. The trustworthiness of the system would also mean that the credentials would be recognized across institutions and borders. Student records and credentials (e.g., diploma, degree, certificate) as well as "micro-credentials" (e.g., certificates from short online courses) could be stored safely on a blockchain-based platform and accessed by other authorized stakeholders. For example, academic institutions and potential employers could view the credentials associated with an individual. Doing so would put the organization ahead of its competitors by supporting a digital credentialing system and minimizing or eliminating fake credentials. However, the ICE Institute had no prior experience in implementing a blockchain-based platform.

ADB through the High-Level Technology Fund under the Supporting the Advanced Knowledge and Skills for Sustainable Growth Project provided technical assistance to the Government of Indonesia in modernizing higher education.[55] Part of this assistance leveraged blockchain to support the ICE Institute in tracking and recording tertiary education student credentials.

The ICE Institute tapped Bina Nusantara University, which is a Jakarta-based private university and has technical resources to support the implementation.[56]

The ICE Institute identified 13 design principles for a national digital credentialing system to guide the development of the system.[57] The key functionalities of the blockchain-based credential system were also identified, along with the high-level user journeys per functionality. Recommendations to develop an MVP followed after a series of meetings, along with a road map of features that can be added to the blockchain-based platform after the MVP is launched.

The ICE Institute opted to use the Ethereum network in anticipation of its future programmability requirements given its built-in smart contract feature. Two layers of blockchain network were used, with certificates issued via a private network using the Ethereum protocol via Kaleido, which developed the blockchain infrastructure system. In the interest of time, Accredible was tapped to provide credential-as-a-service in issuing blockchain-notarized certificates to make it compatible with the blockchain-based platform. This approach was taken as a precursor to shifting to Blockcert, an open standard for creating, issuing, and verifying blockchain-based digital certificates and credentials (footnote 56).

The digital credentialing system that was launched allowed students to source credit-bearing online courses from the ICE Institute. Blockchain enabled the ICE Institute to offer transferable online courses, which were linked to the registration and verification credit system in higher educational institutions. The system was also intended to support linkage to the job market to make school-to-work transition smoother and to improve jobs and skills matching. The ICE Institute aimed to upgrade the system to a Blockcert-based system so that there would no longer be any need for a third-party provider for the digital credentialing system (footnote 56).

---

55 ADB. Indonesia: Supporting the Advanced Knowledge and Skills for Sustainable Growth Project.

56 H. Fathony, P. Pannen, and M.T. Anggoro. 2024. Blockchain in Education: The Journey of Indonesia Cyber Education (ICE) Institute. In P. Pannen and M. Adning, eds. *MOOCs in Asian Higher Education*. Universitas Terbuka. pp. 309–331.

57 The 13 principles were user-centricity, decentralization, inclusion and accessibility, openness, transparency, resilience, reusability, qualifications as a public good, modularity, stackability and portability, and longevity.

58 ADB Southeast Asia Development Solutions. 2022. The Promise of Blockchain in the New Paradigm for Skills Development. 18 February.

Figure 13: How Blockchain Can Be Leveraged for Academic Credential Issuance and Verification

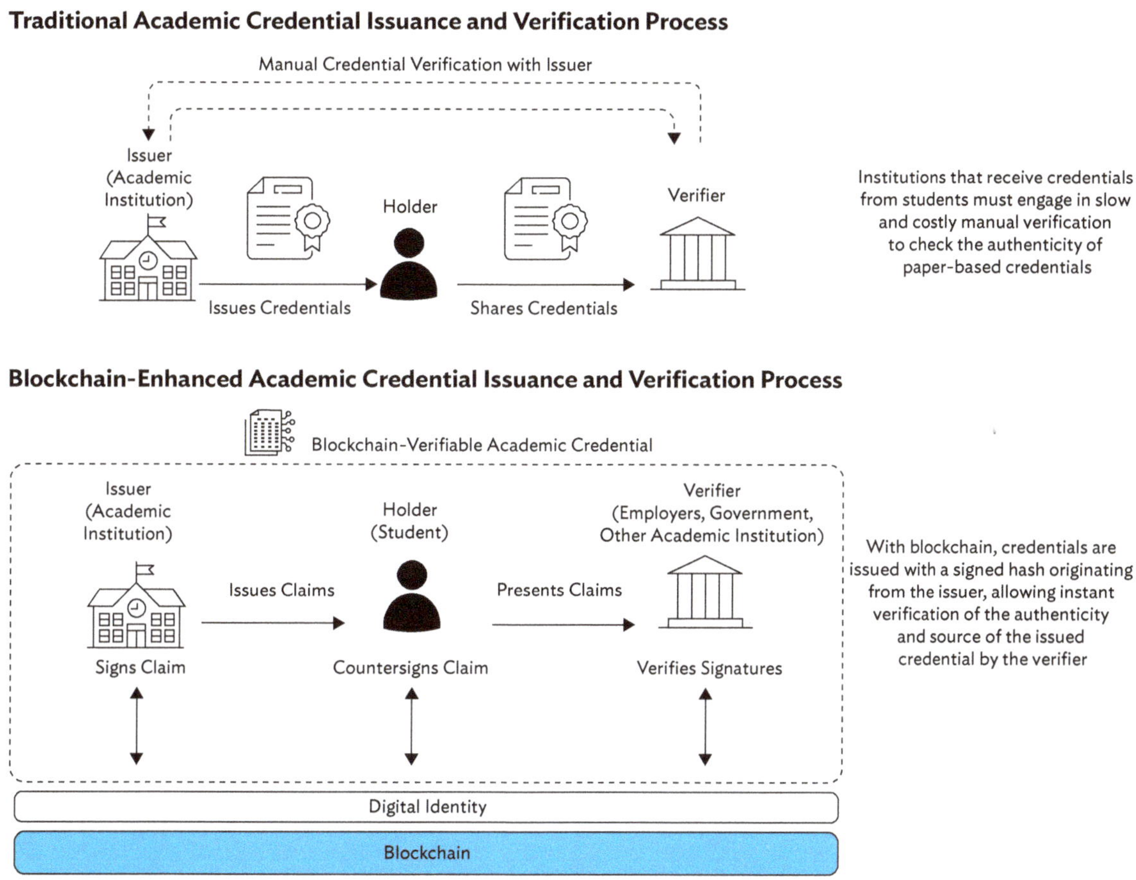

Note: Blockchain can enhance the credentialing system by storing all student records, allowing stakeholders to verify a student's course credits and qualifications in a secure and immutable system.

Source: Asian Development Bank.

Blockchain for development: past and future. Thought leaders from the Asian Development Bank and industry share key insights on the opportunities and risks of blockchain for development.

CHAPTER 5
Insights on Blockchain from Thought Leaders

This chapter presents excerpts from thought leaders on the transformative potential and risks of blockchain in addressing development challenges across Asia and the Pacific. Most were previously published in the Asian Development Blog or Development Asia and explore how blockchain can help leapfrog outdated systems, foster inclusion, and enhance transparency, trust, and efficiency across sectors and use cases. They also highlight the risks and challenges in leveraging blockchain its full development potential. The last entry is from David E. Rutter, chief executive officer and founder of R3, who shares his thoughts on blockchain's continuing role in development.

Four Ways Blockchain Will Disrupt the Energy Sector

In the last 5 years or so, so-called "disruptive" technologies—such as distributed renewable energy, smart grids, energy storage, and fuel cells—have clearly impacted the energy world.

While energy professionals are still adjusting to the new reality, let's take a look at blockchain, an emerging yet potentially even more disruptive technology discussed during a seminar on advanced clean technology solutions for development at ADB's recent Annual Meeting in Yokohama, Japan.

Blockchain is a game-changer, according to Don Tapscott, a TED Talk speaker and one of the world's leading thinkers on the economic and social impact of technology.

"The technology likely to have the greatest impact on the next few decades has arrived. It's not social media. It's not Big Data. It's not robotics. It's not even artificial intelligence. It's called blockchain." said Tapscott.

So, what does the somewhat obscure term "blockchain" mean exactly? How might it affect the future of energy systems? And how will this technology impact ADB's lending and technical assistance operations in developing Asia?

Continue reading at https://blogs.adb.org/blog/4-ways-blockchain-will-disrupt-energy-sector.

This blog post outlines how blockchain will disrupt the energy sector: by enabling peer-to-peer energy trading, improving transparency and efficiency in energy transactions, enhancing grid management through decentralized systems, and supporting the integration of renewable energy sources—all contributing to a more democratized, decentralized, and decarbonized energy future.

This piece was written by Yongping Zhai, former chief of ADB's Energy Sector Group, and was originally published in June 2017.

> *"To grasp blockchain's impact, you might want to use the 5 Ds as a memory aid. It is technology that is digitalized, deregulated, decentralized, distributed, and democratized... By including blockchain and other advanced technologies, ADB's energy sector operations can have even greater development impacts. It can also push developing countries in Asia and the Pacific toward the all-important 6th D – decarbonization of the economy.*
>
> *—Yongping Zhai*

Blockchain Pilots Making Waves in Developing Asia

Blockchain pilots are making waves in developing countries in Asia for two reasons.

The first reason is that most developing countries don't have legacy systems that need to be replaced. Blockchain can provide the first upgrade of an existing inefficient system, or introduce infrastructure that didn't exist before.

The second reason for the widespread interest stems from the light regulatory infrastructure in many countries. So far, this has been an opportunity, but it also raises some concerns as this technology matures.

ADB can play an important role in ensuring that blockchain is implemented in a development-friendly way. We can bring together regulators, best practices, IT experts, and officials to ensure everyone is on the same page.

Continue reading at https://blogs.adb.org/blog/blockchain-pilots-making-waves-developing-asia.

The piece explains how blockchain can revolutionize access to finance by enabling secure, peer-to-peer transactions without intermediaries, making it an is especially transformative technology for unbanked and underserved populations.

This blog post was written by Alisa DiCaprio, former ADB research economist at the ADB Institute, and Steven Beck, advisor on trade and supply chain and finance at ADB's Private Sector Operations Department.

> *"Finance in general and trade finance in particular, is one of the more active areas for blockchain development. Commercial banks throughout the region are participating in consortiums to come up with blockchain solutions to the very expensive, slow, and opaque trade process.*
>
> *—Alisa DiCaprio, Steven Beck*

How Blockchain can Revolutionize Access to Finance

With great change, however, comes great responsibility. Such disruptive technological innovations pose serious regulatory challenges.

While the focus needs to be on establishing a dynamic and enabling market, regulators must nonetheless strive to strike the right balance between regulatory oversight and innovation, as well as ensuring consumer protection.

It is crucial that regulators build and retain trust in the system. They can do this by applying test-and-learn regulatory sandbox approaches, which have proven useful for the fintech industry in various jurisdictions.

This sandbox allows a regulator to "endorse" a promising entity so it can test on a limited scale a new but perhaps uncertain, or unclassified, product, and then assess the benefits and risks. A wave of central banks across the region have already or will soon launch regulatory sandboxes.

Clearly, blockchain and digital ledger technologies have wide-reaching implications across sectors and industries and around the world. Yet, its promise is perhaps biggest in less-developed regions.

Continue reading at https://blogs.adb.org/blog/how-blockchain-can-revolutionize-access-finance.

The piece dives into how some countries in Asia and the Pacific are testing blockchain to develop context-specific solutions to solve their respective development challenges.

This blog post was written by Lotte Schou-Zibell, former ADB finance sector advisor, and was published in September 2017.

"If you have not yet heard of blockchain, you will soon. Blockchain is expected to further speed the pace of change in a financial sector already probing new frontiers. This emerging digital technology promises to also further expand financial inclusion to some of the remotest corners of the planet.

—Lotte Schou-Zibell

How to Turn Blockchain Fintech Hype into Reality

I was wrong to think that financial technology (fintech) would automatically reduce financing gaps. Blockchain, as well as other applications for fintech, has the potential to solve lots of problems.

But we're not there, yet. Despite the billions of dollars invested, all the POCs and the excited news stories, blockchain pilots by and large have not been mainstreamed.

Basic infrastructure needs to be put in place before the hype can meet reality, before we see blockchain fintech solve persistent problems—namely transparency and financial inclusion, including at small and medium-sized enterprises (SMEs)—that hold back growth and job creation.

Amid the fog of hype, we need to be careful to steer this in a meaningful direction, one that will benefit society. Contrary to what many of us originally thought would unfold, there is no evidence to suggest fintech is improving financial inclusion and participation in the global economy, or reducing financing gaps among SMEs.

ADB's 2017 Trade Finance Gaps, Growth, and Jobs Survey bears this out: there is no evidence to support the idea that fintech is reducing gaps. No question – where implemented, it's reducing cost and gaining efficiency; those are good outcomes, but we can now see that reducing cost is not the boon to inclusion and to SME finance that we once thought.

Continue reading at https://blogs.adb.org/blog/how-turn-blockchain-fintech-hype-reality.

This blog post recommends building foundational infrastructure—like digital standards, interoperability, and legal clarity—to enable reliable due diligence and performance tracking and enable blockchain to be leveraged in financial technology so that it goes beyond mere hype.

This blog post was written by Steven Beck, advisor on trade and supply chain and finance ADB's Private Sector Operations Department. The piece was published in October 2017.

> *The hype is fun and dreaming is important, but to catch up with reality we need to develop some basic infrastructure. Creating digital standards for trade, rules for digitization, and achieving global adoption of one harmonized legal identity for companies will create the infrastructure required to move blockchain fintech further.*
>
> *—Steven Beck*

A Promising But Bumpy Road Ahead for Blockchain

Do you remember the world before the internet? Can you imagine your life without it? Prepare yourself, because another revolutionary technology is about to become just as indispensable.

I'm talking about blockchain technology. Blockchain is a digital, distributed ledger that keeps a record of all transactions across participating peer-to-peer networks. It can also be understood as a decentralized database that continuously updates digital records of who owns what, which is then shared within a group or distributed publicly.

It is clear that blockchain is the next generation of the internet. Starting out as interconnected networks for information sharing, the internet grew to connect people for greater collaboration and knowledge sharing by providing access to endless data and information.

Blockchain adds another layer by allowing exchange and storage of "value." By enabling authentication and nearly instant reconciliation of digital transactions, it provides a platform for creating a market (rather than just for exchange of information) between two or more complete strangers without mediators or central authorities.

From an economist's point of view, the main attraction of this technology is its promise for frictionless markets and perfect information. The efficiency gains from getting rid of middlemen in all economic transactions would be huge.

Continue reading at https://blogs.adb.org/blog/promising-bumpy-road-ahead-blockchain.

This blog post argues that blockchain has the transformative potential to create frictionless markets and eliminate information asymmetry, which could yield massive efficiency gains—especially in financial transactions. However, it also notes that there are technical, regulatory, and adoption hurdles that need to be overcome for the full promise of the technology to be realized.

Cyn-Young Park, director of the Regional Cooperation and Integration and Trade Division at ADB's Climate Change and Sustainable Development Department, wrote the blog post, which was published in December 2017.

Like the dotcom bubble in the 1990s, there is much hype over blockchain's potential. But just like any new technology, blockchain applications need to stand the test of time, and will experience numerous failures doing so.

—Cyn-Young Park

How Blockchain Can Rebuild Consumer Trust in Insurance

Insurance, which plays a critical enabling role in wealth creation and economic growth, seems to lack the trust of Asian consumers. Unfortunately, it doesn't seem like this will change anytime soon.

Lack of trust plays a part in the region's extraordinarily high levels of underinsurance. Without the ready availability of insurance products and services to all segments of society, the economic progress made by individuals and households in developing Asia will remain tenuous.

However, the advent of new technologies could help to restore consumer faith in insurance products. One of them—blockchain—has the potential to impact the entire insurance value chain end-to-end.

In fact, harnessing the power of blockchain could transform the way insurers create products, making them more relevant and appealing to the next generation of policyholders.

By creating new gauges of trustworthiness as well as disrupting the existing trust protocols, it promises to provide a secure, transparent and verifiable mechanism to execute transactions—replacing the traditional notion of utmost good faith with provable good faith.

Continue reading at https://blogs.adb.org/blog/how-blockchain-can-rebuild-consumer-trust-insurance.

This blog post presents the idea of how blockchain can transform the insurance industry by replacing traditional notions of trust with transparent and verifiable mechanisms. Blockchain, through smart contracts, secure data sharing, and decentralized storage, can streamline claims, reduce costs, and enhance consumer confidence, even in areas where populations are underinsured.

This piece was written by Arup Kumar Chatterjee, principal finance sector specialist at ADB's Finance Sector Office, Sectors Department 3. The blog post was published in April 2018.

> *By leveraging blockchain, ADB's developing member countries can expand financial inclusion to increase the productivity and earnings of small enterprises.*
>
> *—Arup Kumar Chatterjee*

Creating Open, Honest Government Through Blockchain

Ten years ago, one of the worst financial crises in modern history led to a breakdown of the global financial system. The crisis showed that records and transaction ledgers sourced from a single central party like the banking industry can be manipulated, with dire consequences.

Fast forward to 2018, a digital age when innovations around cryptocurrency, Big Data, and artificial intelligence are challenging traditional business models. Among the array of disruptive technologies existing today, blockchain stands out because it facilitates a new type of interaction that drives transparency in transactions.

Blockchain technology allows for multiple-entry bookkeeping in a system that requires consensus among parties to validate each transaction. Every record is verified, encrypted, and stored permanently to ensure its immutability.

By design, blockchain is maintained by a host of different computer nodes independent from each other, but in agreement about every transactions. In the absence of a gatekeeper, blockchain inspires enough confidence for people to trust the data presented in a chain of encrypted records and distributed across a network.

The bedrock of blockchain is decentralization: control is democratized and trust is distributed. There is such tremendous interest on this technology's potential that there now seems to be a blockchain for everything—from trading markets to supply chain management.

So, how can this technology be also applied to renew trust in government transactions? In fact, it is already happening.

Continue reading at https://blogs.adb.org/blog/creating-open-honest-government-through-blockchain.

This blog post presents the idea that blockchain can restore public trust in government by ensuring transparency, security, and immutability in public records and transactions. It highlights pilot projects like Fiji's land records system, showing how decentralized technology can eliminate gatekeepers and reduce manipulation in governance.

This piece was written by Chee Anne Roño, an ADB consultant. The blog post was published in July 2018.

> *If the technology continues to evolve at present pace, blockchain could play a key role in eliminating mistrust in public records and government transactions. Using the best available technology to renew public trust in this increasingly digital world could accelerate growth and inclusiveness – the hallmark of smart development.*
>
> *—Chee Anne Roño*

How Blockchain Can Improve Supply Chain Transparency in Maldives

Maldives is exploring the use of high-level technologies to support a national single window system that will make it faster and more efficient to trade with other countries in South Asia and beyond.

Backed by ADB's High-Level Technology Fund, the South Asia Subregional Economic Cooperation National Single Window Project will pilot the use of blockchain technology to improve trade facilitation and supply chain management.

The High-Level Technology Fund supports the introduction of advanced digital technologies in international trade to improve trustworthiness, efficiency, and timeliness of local and regional supply chains.

Maldives is one of the smallest countries in Asia and the Pacific by population and land area. Its estimated population of 436,330 is widely dispersed over 187 inhabited islands across an archipelago that is more than 800 kilometers long and 130 kilometers wide. Despite its geographical challenges, Maldives has successfully developed many islands into high-end tourist resorts. Strong growth in tourism and tourism-related activities helped the country attain middle-income status in 2010.

Like many small island economies, Maldives relies heavily on imports for food, fuel, and other goods, while exports—primarily of fresh fish and fish products—have been increasing.

A single window for trade can reduce delays and lower costs associated with the clearance of goods while maintaining the needed controls over fees and duties on imports or exports. The national single window is designed to interface with existing systems of cross border regulatory agencies, Malé Seaport, and Velana International Airport. It will address key bottlenecks to international trade procedures. An automated single window system will be established and made operational, and capacity building and competency on its operations will be developed under the project.

Continue reading at https://development.asia/explainer/how-blockchain-can-improve-supply-chain-transparency-maldives.

This blog post introduces a blockchain use case in Maldives, which tested the technology's potential to streamline trade.

This piece was written by Takeru Toba, who was an economist working in ADB's South Asia Department, and Lin Lu, advisor and head of the Information Access Unit, Office of the Secretary at ADB. The blog post was published in April 2020.

> *The technology is expected to make the documentation process and parcel tracking in cross-border trade more efficient and reliable.*
>
> *—Takeru Toba, Lin Lu*

Driving Sustainable Development Through Real-World Asset Tokenization on Public Blockchain Platforms

David E. Rutter, Executive Chair and Founder at R3

Blockchain is powering the next evolution of financial markets through the tokenization of real-world assets (RWAs). For too long, RWAs have been issued onto networks that are unable to communicate with one another, hampering the very utility gains that blockchain is intended to provide.

More efficient financial products and services are crucial to reducing costs and lowering barriers to adoption for individuals and institutions operating in developing economies. As internet capital markets grow, institutions will no longer need to choose between private control and public reach—they will be able to operate on public networks with the standards of compliance and privacy they expect, while tapping into liquidity, yield, and performance that private environments alone cannot deliver.

Public blockchain networks will make transacting across borders faster, cheaper, and more efficient than ever. DeFi-native innovations like lending pools can unlock financing opportunities for entrepreneurs and SMEs, ushering in new capital and providing infrastructure for local investors to more effectively deploy capital. Access to stablecoin-based savings products and RWA-backed yield vaults can provide enhanced opportunities for hedging against domestic currency risks. This can also support economic development through investment in local assets, including private credit funds or local trade financing.

The industry is at an inflexion point, as greater regulatory clarity and successful live implementations boost market confidence in blockchain technology and RWA tokenization. With investors increasingly seeking diversified yield and institutional firms looking to access the benefits of public chains, the demand for high-quality tokenized assets will continue to grow. Initiatives that bridge private and public blockchains are key to spurring RWA adoption, broadening access to financial markets, and creating new market opportunities.

www.ingramcontent.com/pod-product-compliance
Lightning Source LLC
Chambersburg PA
CBHW041759220926
51847CB00014B/252
* 9 7 8 9 2 9 2 7 7 7 8 5 2 *